Modern Education

One Size Fits All

The Gentle Wind Series

THE PSYCHOLOGY OF SPIRITUAL GROWTH

MODERN RELIGION & THE DESTRUCTION
OF SPIRITUAL CAPACITY

MODERN EDUCATION:
ONE SIZE FITS ALL

THE FAILURE AND DISUNITY
OF THE AMERICAN WAY

Modern Education

One Size Fits All

Channelled from the Brotherhood
by Mary E. Carreiro

A Gentle Wind Book
Volume III

Bergin & Garvey Publishers, Inc
Massachusetts

First published in 1988 by
Bergin & Garvey Publishers, Inc.
670 Amherst Road
South Hadley, Massachusetts 01075

89   987654321

Manufactured in the United States of America

Library of Congress Cataloging-in-Publication Data

Carreiro, Mary Elizabeth
  Modern education: one size fits all / channelled from the Brotherhood by Mary E. Carreiro.

    p. cm.
  "A Gentle Wind book, volume III."
  ISBN 0-89789-169-4: $29.95. ISBN 0-89789-168-6 (pbk.): $10.95
  1. Education   2. New Age movement.   3. Spiritual life.   4. Brotherhood (Brothers and Sisters of the Inner World)   I. Title.
  LA217.C38   1988
  370'.973—dc19   88-2861
                                                                              CIP

Photo Credits: Byron F. Greatorex, pages 5, 8, 9, 11 and 16; others by Gentle Wind staff.

Contents

READERS CAN BE ASSURED *that the information contained in this book does not come from the human world. It has been telepathically communicated to humanity by the Brotherhood. It contains less than one percent of what We could tell humanity about modern education. We could fill several reference rooms of the New York Public Library with data on this subject alone. We are giving humanity this initial amount of data only to see how the information will be used.*

Introduction

THIS IS A BOOK about modern education. More importantly, it is a book about reality. It is the true story of what happens to human beings when they are removed from contact with the outside world and incarcerated in classrooms for twelve years or more. It is an account of what occurs when a young adult is released from this incarceration and then faced with the reality of finding a spouse, having a baby, raising children, caring for a sick parent, or grieving the death of a friend or family member.

This is a story of the effects on the human mind when it is forced to memorize large quantities of useless, meaningless information. It is about what happens to people when they try to study electricity from science books without ever locating the fuse boxes or circuit breakers in their own homes. It is about how people view the physical world when they are taught to believe that welding, carpentry, and auto mechanics should be reserved for school failures and potential dropouts.

This is a factual chronicle of the consequences to a society when the vast majority of its people have been so educated that they can no longer repair the things they need to support their daily survival. It is about how that society chooses its political leaders when the citizens have spent twelve or more years submitting to the authority of teachers who are generally devoid of real character or values. It is about the repercussions to that society's economy and manufacturing base when the business school graduates gain control of the nation's major companies.

This is also a book about souls. It is about how the spiritual part of a person is affected when the human part is denied the opportunity to interact with the world in a natural way. It is an accounting of what happens to people's souls when the human part of them cannot establish the proper connections between cause and effect.

This book, like the preceding volumes in this series, has been given to humanity by the Brotherhood under the direction of the Logos of this planet. (The Brotherhood is a group of souls, both men and women, who are dedicated to the spiritual growth of humanity.) Because these books are about reality, they do not make for pleasant reading. They are devastating to most healthy ego structures; and, at the same time, they are useless to people who cannot be devastated in some way. Most people who read this book will feel the way healthy parents would feel if they discovered that their child had suddenly died. Nothing can be done to recover the child. The parents are angry, shocked, and hurt at the one who tells them of their child's death, no matter how compassionate that newsbearer might be.

The Brotherhood knows the heartache that people feel when they first discover reality. The Brotherhood offers these books with the same compassion the newsbearer feels when he or she speaks to the parents who have lost their child. Like the newsbearer who knows that the parents must be told the truth about their child, the Brotherhood sees how desperate humanity is to know about reality. If there was an easier way to reconnect the human race to reality, the Brotherhood would use it. However, humanity has been so lost for so long that there is no other way.

This book will not cause evolution, nor will it provide a set of guidelines to people who claim that they want to grow. Humanity is not yet ready to resume the process of spiritual evolution. To write a book about how to accomplish evolution would be like trying to teach people how to paint the final trim on a house before they have even cleared a plot of land on which to build. The initial books in this series are only about clearing the land, because most people do not even know they have a house to build.

Most readers will want to complain that this book is too negative. In fact, the problems created by modern education are much worse than we can portray in this book. What readers will be discovering is that reality is very negative. However, most people have constructed their lives on the illusion that the world is a positive place. The New Age spiritual types thrive on this disturbed illusion, which is why so many of them continue to suffer from mental-emotional problems despite all of their espoused spiritual pursuits. To maintain this fantasy, most readers, especially the spiritual types, will want to discredit this book as being too negative. In these cases, it would be more honest to simply close the book and throw it away than to waste one's valuable spiritual resources on futile attempts to discredit reality.

At the beginning of each chapter, We have included a short reminder that this book is about reality. This is actually a very positive book in that it is the only book in the world today which challenges the tyrannical and abusive methods of modern education. Any reader who has ever sat in a classroom could give testimony to the fact that this book is accurate and true. But people cannot give such testimony and also maintain the illusion that the world is a positive place. This is why We will continue to remind them that present-day reality is extremely negative and foul.

For all readers, some of their most sacred and dangerous ideas about education will be challenged. We will expose both the human and the spiritual tragedies that occur every day in modern classrooms. We tell of many things that humanity is not yet prepared to change. This book is here now to lay the foundations for a later time when such change will be possible, provided that people are willing to be responsible for discovering reality now.

Any suggestions contained within this book for an alternative form of education should not be taken as descriptive of an ideal educational system. These suggestions only refer to a possible interim system. This interim system would give humanity an opportunity to be healed from damages inflicted by the current system so that schools could eventually be established that would truly serve each person.

Before humanity can begin to establish an effective and positive way of educating children, the interim system would need to be functioning for a minimum of five generations. To be adequately healed from the destruction inflicted by today's system, humanity must reach a point where no one alive can remember anything about that system. Even great, great grandparents must only have

memories of the interim system before the damage will be suffi-
ciently repaired to go on to a better way.

The suggestions contained in this book are actually quite inferior
to the design and structure of an ideal educational system. They
should be viewed as more of a stopgap measure to alleviate the
current holocaust created by modern education and as a bridge to
something much, much better. However, because people have been
living in darkness for so long, they are not prepared for anything
better. Most people are like children who were born in concentration camps. They have known no other reality so they assume that
growing up in a concentration camp is a positive experience. They
are not prepared, as yet, for life outside the concentration camp
and would not know what to do in a world that was very much
improved.

The problems caused by modern education are much more damaging and tragic than We can describe in one volume. There are
at least five more volumes that could be written merely to adequately describe the seriousness and the extent of the damage
caused by the current educational system. We could write an entire
volume on *the destructive effects of grading and testing on the
human consciousness;* another on *the damage caused to the mental vehicles through the educational process;* and another about
*the annihilation of all natural human instinct occurring daily in
schools.* We could also offer a volume describing *the complete
inferiority of the educational system* that would be laughable if it
were not so tragic, and a final book describing *the spiritual holocaust of modern education.*

These books will not be written, because it is not Our job to
correct the backward and hurtful systems that people have come
to worship and admire. We have given humanity this book and
the others in the Gentle Wind series only to get people started.
Our job is to help humanity return to a path of spiritual evolution.
However, most people are too destroyed by religion and education
to be able to seek spiritual growth without the resources of the
Brotherhood. Even with this help many simply cannot recover from
the damage which has been inflicted by religion and education.
This book is a key to humanity's release from darkness. Unfortunately, most people have been incarcerated for so long that they
do not even realize they are captives.

1

THE MEDIUM IS THE MESSAGE

NOTE: This is a book about reality. Reality is not positive. Reality is extremely negative.

IT SEEMS ONLY APPROPRIATE for a book about modern education to begin with a short quiz. This quiz was designed to help you, the reader, begin to understand exactly what happened to you during all of those years in classrooms. This is not the kind of quiz that you can either pass or fail. It is not even the kind of quiz that can be answered with your mind, no matter how mentally gifted you might be. The answers to these questions are all self-evident because they are about reality as it exists without any falsification. If you relate to reality, you will have no difficulty with the quiz.

Before taking this short picture test, it is important to understand something about how human beings work. The medium, for all human beings, is always the message. This means that the subject being taught in the classroom is not nearly as important as the person who is teaching the subject, and how that subject is being taught.

For example, when Mrs. Smith sees her oldest son Robbie hit his younger brother, she runs over to Robbie, slaps him across the

1

head and says, "Don't hit your brother." Robbie does not learn to stop hitting his brother when he is slapped on the head. He actually learns more about the use of physical violence because the medium is always the message.

When Mrs. Smith was a little girl, her father hit her whenever he thought she needed to be disciplined. Sometimes, Mrs. Smith feels guilty when she hits her children, particularly when she remembers the minister telling her that parents should not beat up their children. Although what the minister tells her causes her to feel guilty, Mrs. Smith does not stop beating up her children because when she was little her father often hit her. That medium was the message.

When children study spelling, science or history in schools, they do not usually remember much about what they are studying. They are much more aware of how they feel in school, and how they are being treated by their teachers. Most adults can usually recall much more about their teachers and how they were treated in school than anything they supposedly learned about science or history in the classroom. Human beings always learn the medium, no matter what words might be contained in any other attempted message.

Because human beings always learn the medium, they also always repeat the medium because this is the only real message. This means that what children learn in school about life has much more to do with how they are being treated than with what they are being taught. It means that when schools confine children to classrooms and then use that confinement as leverage to make the students behave in certain ways, children are really learning about the leverage of confinement. Therefore, all of the non-reality oriented behaviors such as memorizing from books and sitting still in chairs all day, have much more of an effect than any of the subjects that are taught.

When children are young, they need to be with people who can and will relate to them. When teachers stand before a group of children every day, with a curriculum of eight subjects to cover, they cannot relate personally and directly with each child. Since the medium is the message, what children learn is that relating is not important. This experience actually prepares them more for watching television, where they can sit in front of more adults who do not relate to them personally, than it does for anything else in life.

As you are taking this quiz remember that the most important decision most people will make in their lives is choosing a spouse. The most significant thing for people is generally their marriage, followed by their relationships with their children. The main purchase in most people's lives will be their home, followed by buying an automobile. The most important psychological need for everyone is peace of mind.

As you go through this quiz be sure to ask yourself how education has directly prepared you for married life and parenthood. Take the time to recall what you learned in school about buying a house and maintaining it, and buying a car and maintaining it. Ask yourself how your education has helped you find peace of mind.

As you answer the questions in this picture quiz, you must remember that the medium is always the message. Otherwise, you will not be properly connected to reality and you will find this quiz more complicated than it really is. You should also notice that the word *DIRECTLY* is underlined. Educated human beings think it is good enough to have something *indirectly* related to something else. This is one of the many inherent dangers in becoming educated. This kind of thinking causes people to bend and distort reality until they are no longer connected to the real world.

How is life in the classroom <u>directly</u> related to . . .

. . . Choosing a compatible spouse?   5

. . . Finding a job?

. . . Building or buying a house?

. . . Having a baby?

. . . *Raising children?*

. . . Fixing your car?

. . . Managing your money?

How is life in the classroom <u>directly</u> related to . . .

. . . *Shopping for food?*

. . . Cooking a meal? 15

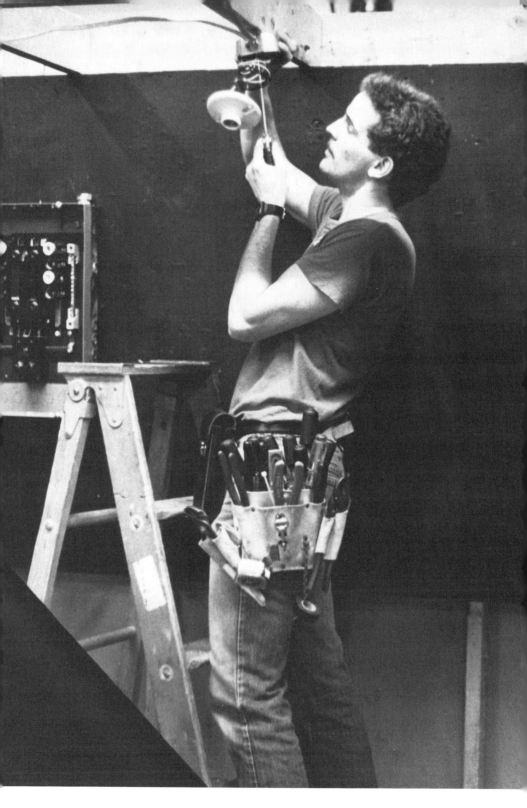

. . . Installing and repairing your electricity?

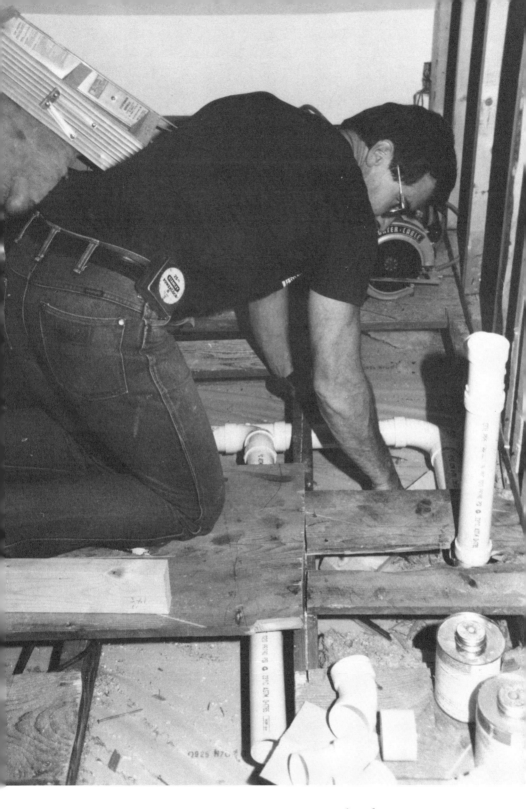

... Installing and repairing your plumbing? 17

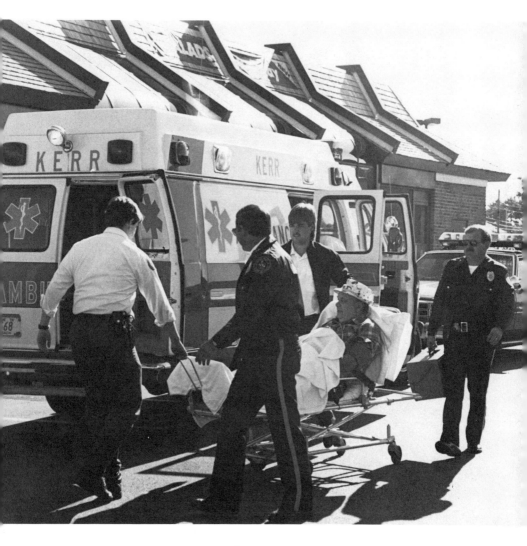

. . . Handling an emergency?

. . . Fixing and flying an airplane!   19

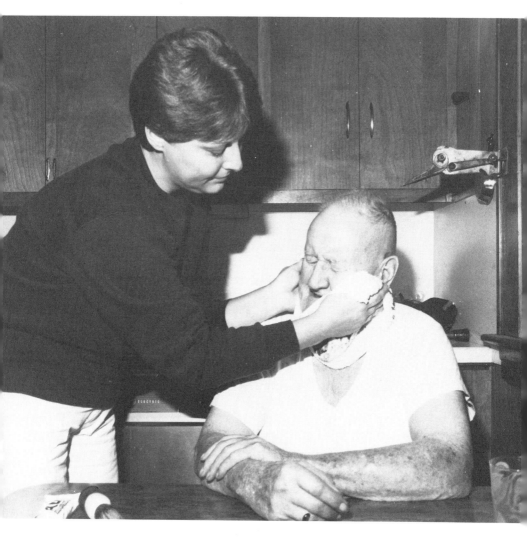

. . . Caring for the elderly?

. . . Facing death?   21

How does life in the classroom
help a person find peace of mind?

2

THE HUMAN TRAGEDY OF MODERN EDUCATION

NOTE: This is a book about reality. Reality is not positive. Reality is extremely negative.

Dick and Jane Go To Grammar School

ONCE UPON A TIME in a small suburb of Detroit, Dick Wilson and his younger sister, Jane, were busily getting ready for school. It was the first day of the school year so everyone was both nervous and excited. Little Jane was particularly nervous because she was about to start first grade. Although Jane had already attended pre-school and kindergarten, she thought that the first grade seemed like a much more important and serious step. Her parents told her that first grade was real school while kindergarten and preschool were just for play. Jane was not sure what to expect and the unknown worried her.

Dick was also feeling a little nervous inside. He was a veteran at age ten, and starting the fourth grade, so he decided that he would not let anyone know how nervous he really felt. Dick was a good student but not the best in his class. His last three teachers had all told him that he could do even better if he would just try a little harder. Once he had overheard his mother tell his aunt that he was not living up to his full potential. Although he had not been exactly sure what those words meant, he was left with the distinct feeling that his parents were not pleased with him.

Both Dick and Jane were wearing new jeans and jerseys, bought especially for the first day of the school year. They each had new lunch boxes. Jane had a bright pink plastic case with a picture of Princess Leia on the front panel, while Dick had a dark green metal box with three large dinosaurs stamped on each side. Mrs. Wilson had packed the boxes with apple juice and snacks, because today was only a half session and the children would not be staying for a regular lunch hour.

Dick and Jane could walk to school since they only lived three blocks away. Most of the other children traveled by bus, and had to leave much earlier in the morning than the Wilson children. Sometimes Dick wished he could ride the school bus, especially when a bus would pass him on route to school and his friends would wave and yell out the windows. However, most of the time he was content to walk.

When it was time to leave for school, Mrs. Wilson kissed the children and then walked them to the end of the driveway. They all waved goodbye several times until Dick and Jane turned the corner to walk up the three blocks to the Emerson Grammar School. Neither Dick nor Jane said anything on the way to school, but each wondered what their new teachers would be like and who would be in their respective classes. Dick recalled a time when he had been caught talking in a lunch line by Mr. Marshall, the cafeteria monitor. Mr. Marshall had made him stand in the middle of the cafeteria until every child had walked through the lunch line. Dick had been more humiliated than he would ever have thought possible. He quickly dismissed this memory and went back to wondering what his day would be like.

The bell rang just as Dick and Jane entered the schoolyard. A voice came over the loudspeaker directing all the new first graders to the far end of the playground. Jane looked over and saw three women standing next to the schoolyard fence. One of them was Mrs. Gardener who had been teaching for over thirty years. She was considered to be very strict with her classes. Some parents felt that her methods were very good for helping young first graders make a quick adjustment to classroom life. Jane hoped that she was not on Mrs. Gardener's list. The other two women were younger and seemed to smile more, and anything would be better than Mrs. Gardener.

By now Mr. Ryan had gathered his twenty-two fourth graders and herded them down the hall. Dick was one of them. Dick had never had a male teacher before. He wondered why there were so many women teachers and so few men. He wondered what Mr. Ryan would be like. Just as they got to the classroom entrance, Mr. Ryan cracked a joke. The whole class was laughing. Although Dick never actually heard the joke, he felt much better and laughed along with the others out of sheer relief.

The day started as usual with the Pledge of Allegiance and the singing of the National Anthem. For Dick, this ritual was strangely comforting. He was not sure what it meant, but it was so familiar that he was relieved to recite and sing just for the familiarity. Jane, on the other hand, was still overwhelmed. She had made it to her new classroom with Ms. Robbins, a very young woman who had only been teaching for six months before this year. Ms. Robbins spoke softly and seemed to be nice, but the children were all so nervous that their combined fears created an extremely tense first few moments. Things got better when Ms. Robbins passed out paper and pencils and told the children to print their names so that she could get to know everyone.

Dick and the other fourth graders had already received their math books. In fact, they were quietly filling in the first ten review pages while Mr. Ryan passed out science books and other supplies. Before the morning ended, Dick would have six books in all, stacked neatly in his desk along with his own pencils and notebook which he had brought from home. None of the books looked very interesting, but Mr. Ryan kept talking about having a good year so Dick decided to wait and see how things turned out.

Jane had settled down and the butterflies in her stomach were gone. It was hard for Jane to be quiet for so long. Her preschool and kindergarten teachers had always let the children talk in class as long as they did not talk too loudly. However, first grade was definitely more serious, and Jane was having a difficult time adjusting to so much silence. She was very glad to hear the dismissal bell at eleven-thirty. She decided that the best part of school was the ten o'clock snack and recess. When she said this to her parents later that day, they both laughed and told Jane that she would like school once she got used to it.

At 11:35 that morning, Dick met Jane on the outer edge of the schoolyard. He tapped her on the head and called her "squirt" the way he always did when he was glad to see her but did not want to admit it. They walked home together without saying much. They each silently recalled different moments during the morning as if to review once more the potential ups and downs of the school year ahead.

Ted and Sally Go To Grammar School

Once upon a time on a planet far away, Ted Johnson and his younger sister Sally were getting dressed for school. It was the first day of the school year and both children were excited about returning to school. Ted, at age eight, was looking forward to learning to read and write. Over the summer Ted had discovered that he wanted to know how to write to his friends from summer camp, and also that he was frustrated because he could not read the directions in an electronics kit his father had given him. There were other things he wanted to know about as well, that he could only get at by learning to read and write.

On Ted's planet, no one was ever forced by law to attend school. Children went to school because school was so interesting and relevant to life on their planet, and very few children ever stayed away. Even those who did always returned eventually. On Ted's planet, children were only taught to read when they were ready to learn. This usually meant that they would begin reading and writing classes around the age of eight, after they had a chance to discover how reading and writing might be useful to them.

No one on Ted's planet ever got graded on anything. Children measured their own levels of accomplishment by comparing their current work to their work done six months earlier. They were always shown projects that demonstrated standards of excellence in each subject, but were never asked to rely on the approval or disapproval of any of their teachers. Usually the children on Ted's planet worked very hard to accomplish their own goals, which were often much higher than the goals that one might imagine their teachers setting for them.

On Ted's planet, students always chose their teachers. No one was ever forced to work with anyone he or she did not like. In fact, teachers were only allowed to work with students they liked and felt good about teaching. Although this system was not perfect, very few children on Ted's planet ever worried about being hurt or humiliated by a teacher. Teachers were people with high standards who wanted the best from the children they were teaching, and they were forbidden by law from humiliating or punishing any student.

Sally, at age six, was enrolled in a program for mostly five to eight year olds. On Ted and Sally's planet, there were no formal desks or rigid classrooms. Children were allowed to talk, to roam about as they pleased, to eat when they got hungry, to rest when they were tired, and to go home when they felt finished with school for the day.

Sally's room was a large barn with different projects set up in various sections of the spacious room. These projects were mostly construction projects that involved the use of sand, clay, paper, wood, and metal. The children were allowed to work on any projects that were of interest to them. The only requirement was for the children to learn about the source of the materials, and how those materials and any special equipment could be used safely. Most projects involved building. Sally was looking forward to starting her woodworking classes. She would be able to use the small scroll saws this year, and she had some great ideas for toys she wanted to make. Her class was also going to build bird houses and set them up in the yard of the learning center. Ted's unit would be photographing the birds when they came to feed.

Both Sally and Ted already knew their teachers. Sally's teacher's name was Max Sawyer. Max taught Sally's class last year, and he would most probably be following the children through high school graduation, which occurred at age fourteen or fifteen for most students. Max was twenty and had just started teaching last year. Sally thought of him as a smarter, older brother and was very fond of him. Max liked Sally as well. He knew about her big brother approach, but found it very supportive.

Both Ted and Sally were dressed in new jeans and jerseys that their mother, Susan, had bought at the high school craft and trade fair. The summer session sewing classes had made a full line of fall clothing for the fair, which yielded a nice profit for the sewing department and probably meant a new computerized sewing machine for this year's classes. Ted and Sally each carried wooden lunch boxes that Ted had made in school last year. Sally had painted hers in greens and blues. Ted had carved a large dinosaur on the front panel of his. Ted and his class had actually gone out into the woods, found a maple tree on a tract of land set for clearing, and chopped down the tree. They had hauled it off in sections to the lumber mill, and there helped turn the tree into usable size boards which were then kiln dried. It had been one of Ted's favorite projects.

When the children were ready to leave for school, Susan Johnson kissed them goodbye and walked them to the end of the driveway. Usually, Ted went to school later in the day. There were no formal class hours and he liked working when the woodworking shop was less crowded. Sally, on the other hand, was an early riser and preferred getting to school when the doors opened.

The teachers worked whenever the children needed assistance with a project, or when a group of children required some instruction about the safe and proper use of school equipment. Children could come and go during the day as long as their parents knew where they were. In fact, the doors of the learning center were open to anyone in town who wanted to visit, watch, or help out with a project. Conversely, the children were required to spend several hours a week finding out about what was going on in their town and surrounding communities. Ted's class would be visiting a home for the elderly throughout the next few weeks, learning how to take care of some of the residents who required assistance with daily activities. Next month they would begin observing the construction of a home located down the road. The blueprints were already hanging on the walls of Ted's workroom so that the children could start to absorb what they would soon see being built.

Ted was glad to see his teacher Anne Martin. She greeted him at the door. Ted spent most of his first day gathering the supplies he and his classmates would need for two large worktables they were going to build for the darkroom. They would need a few consultations with Bill Simpson, the shop instructor, but they felt confident that they could design and build something worthwhile. Ted was so busy organizing his work area that he did not notice it was almost four-thirty. Mr. Simpson came in to let the boys and girls know that it was time to start cleaning up for the day. Ted and his friends cleared the work area of the day's dust and trash so they would be ready to continue the project tomorrow. Sally had gone home earlier, so Ted walked home alone, mentally planning the work he would do the next day.

Dick and Jane Go To High School

Once upon a time in that same suburb of Detroit, Dick Wilson and his younger sister, Jane, were busily getting ready for school. It was the first day of the school year and Jane's first day in high school. Jane was nervous about going to high school, but she thought that it might be fun to go to the high school parties and date some of the upperclassmen. Jane was enrolled in the college preparatory course but she was not sure about what to actually expect from school. She knew that the "smart kids" took college prep, the "dumb kids" took business and secretarial courses, and the real flunkies took industrial arts. She was glad to be in the smart group because they were also the most popular kids in school and seemed to be having the most fun.

Dick was starting his senior year. He was, again, the veteran student who knew where and with whom to hang out. He was still not the best student in his class but he was in the top twenty of almost two hundred students. Most of his high school teachers really liked him. He was smart enough to please his teachers without being so smart that he alienated his friends. Dick worried about school just the same. He worried about making mistakes and looking foolish, since he prided himself on being just "cool" enough to be popular. Occasionally he cheated on exams when he did not have time to study, or was just not interested in the subject. However, most of the time he did his homework and passed his tests on his memory, which was quite good.

Although it was only seven-fifteen in the morning, Jane had already been up for almost two hours. She had awakened early so that she could spend extra time on her hair and makeup. She was wearing her new designer jeans and a yellow-and-white print blouse bought especially for this day with some of the babysitting money she had earned during the summer. Like Jane, Dick also spent some extra time fussing over his own hair, and shaving a little more carefully than usual so as not to cut himself in any unsightly way. This did not stop him, however, from teasing Jane about her efforts to appear attractive to the new high school boys.

Jane gathered her pocketbook and a few school supplies and headed for the bus stop. Dick waited in the driveway for his friend Zeke to pick him up. Soon Zeke pulled up in the Ford Mustang that his father had helped him buy this summer. Zeke had washed and waxed the car for the occasion and had purchased his favorite tapes to play in the newly-installed tape deck.

Matt Willis and Jim Michelson were already in the back seat smoking their usual morning dosage of marijuana and talking about the really "good stuff" they could get for the weekend. Dick took his obligatory hit and then passed the joint back to Matt and Jim. Dick used enough drugs to be popular, but unlike Matt and Jim he was not a serious daily user. He rarely ventured into pills or cocaine, although he knew plenty of kids who did and thought it to be quite normal.

Jane's school bus pulled up just behind Zeke's car, so Dick and Jane entered the high school building at the same time but did not acknowledge their relationship to one another in any way. Dick went off to his homeroom where Mr. Clemens was waiting for his section of senior class students. Mr. Clemens was also the senior math instructor, so Dick would be meeting with him at least twice a day. Mr. Clemens had the reputation of being one of the more unpleasant teachers. He tended to favor the boys, however, and Dick was relieved to be among the males in this class.

Dick would be taking six subjects this semester, including advanced calculus with Mr. Clemens. He would also be taking physics, American history, English literature, music, and French. Nothing on this menu particularly interested Dick, but he supposed that he could bear it for one more year, especially the senior year which tended to be somewhat shorter than other years. He also decided that things were looking even better when he discovered that Melissa Shapiro was in two of his six classes. He thought that Melissa had the best body of any girl in the senior class.

Jane and the other ninth-graders were sent to the school auditorium for orientation and class assignments. The principal gave a long lecture on the value of a high school education. Most of the students could not wait for him to finish but everyone was polite enough not to start any trouble on the first day. When he finished, the students lined up according to their assigned section numbers and then marched off to class.

Jane was assigned to Ms. Pearl's homeroom. Ms. Pearl was one of the oldest teachers in the school. Her classes were notoriously noisy because her hearing was failing and she could not hear the students talking during her profoundly boring history lectures. Jane was upset at the idea of having to spend part of her first year with Ms. Pearl, but students were never allowed to choose their teachers so Jane was pretty much stuck with the old Pearl for the year ahead.

Jane would also be taking six subjects, including algebra, Spanish or French, English grammar, science, history, and a combination of home economics and music appreciation, which were split into half-year courses. Jane, like Dick, was not very excited about anything on her schedule, but she did not think much about her disappointment because it just seemed like that was the way things were.

The day went by fairly quickly, as the newness of returning to school had not yet diminished. At two o'clock, the dismissal bell rang. Jane ran for the bus while Dick and his friends met at Zeke's car. On the ride home they each thought about the day and pondered their homework assignments, which included covering the outside of all their textbooks for the year in something to protect the books from wear and weather. Jane wondered why there was so much fuss about covering books which would only be used next year by another group of disinterested students.

Ted and Sally Go To High School

Once upon a time on a planet far away, Ted Johnson and his younger sister Sally were getting dressed for school. It was the first day of the school year and both Ted and Sally were excited about returning to school. Ted, now fifteen-and-a-half, would be graduating sometime during this year. Ted was actually one of the older seniors because he had decided to take an additional year of boatbuilding. Over the summer he had spent a month with a boatwright on an island near his home. He had helped work on an eighteen-foot fishing boat and was then allowed to venture out on the boat's first fishing cruise. Ted had a lot of new ideas about boats that he would like to build and could hardly wait for school to start so he could get his next boat under construction.

Ted had started building boats almost three years ago in his advanced woodworking class. He had discovered at that time that he was going to need math. He needed to learn geometry in order to fit all the two-angle, trapezoid, and parallelogram-shaped parts into his boats. He wanted to understand calculus to do the celestial navigation that would be necessary to sail or motor the boats. He had also taken the appropriate mechanics courses to rebuild and repair small boat engines so that he would be able to get his boat moving again should he ever experience engine failure.

In Ted's high school, no one was ever allowed to take courses unless those courses had a specific use and purpose in the person's life. Children usually started high school at age twelve and graduated at fourteen or fifteen. During these years they were required to take courses in accounting and economics that involved life experiences like balancing a checkbook, filling out tax returns, and applying for mortgages through local banks. They had to learn about the electrical systems in their homes, and each of them spent several months apprenticing with a carpenter, electrician, welder, plumber, and auto mechanic. Everyone chose certain areas of interest and then developed their own curriculum around those interests.

All students were expected to learn about pregnancy and to attend a birth if possible. Everyone was required to learn how to care for infants, toddlers, and older children as well as how to provide for someone who was ill and bedridden. Everyone needed to learn one other language, and to spend one month in a country where people spoke that language. If students wanted to study art, music, or photography, these and many other subjects were also available.

Sally was starting high school this year, although on her planet there were no clear distinctions between schools or grade levels. She would be taking all the basic courses in electricity, plumbing, welding, and carpentry. Thus far, she had enjoyed welding the most, although she had only done gas welding with a small tank. Sally was interested in metal sculptures which appealed to her artistic nature. She was also interested in bridge construction, both design and function. Last summer she had worked with a crew repairing a highway bridge on the other side of her town. She did not get to do much welding, but she did have the chance to watch some real experts at work. Her best friend, Harry, was also interested in welding. He repaired all the broken shop equipment for the school, and had a small machinery business in his home.

Both Ted and Sally were anxious to get back into their projects at school. Neither Ted nor Sally fussed much about their hair or clothes, although they were both neat and appropriately dressed.

They usually wore overalls or painter's pants because they were sure to get glue, paint, oil, or some other stains on themselves in the course of the day. They were also too busy with their projects to spend too much time on their hair and wardrobe. They had both tried marijuana. Ted had found that it interfered with his ability to remain alert in the shop. He decided not to bother with drugs because they prevented him from doing what he wanted to do most. In fact, hardly anyone on Ted and Sally's planet bothered with drugs. They simply did not have the time or interest.

When it was time to leave for school, Ted went out to wait for his friend Zach. Zach had an electric car that he and four other boys had built over the previous few years. The car was very slow. All the builders took turns driving. It was Zach's week to drive, so he had promised Ted a ride on the first day of school. Although Zach was only fifteen, on his planet anyone over fourteen could apply for a license. The accident rates were very low since most children started to learn about cars at age twelve. By fourteen, they were expected to be responsible, competent adults—an expectation which these young adults met with ease.

Ted thought about his teacher, Anne Martin, and how much he would miss her after he left for college. She had become a deep and trusted friend, someone on whom he could rely. When he got to school that morning, he went directly to the shop to begin his boat. Anne was waiting to welcome him back to school, and he realized again how important she had been to him. Then he began to lay out his plans for a ten-foot lapstrake sailboat.

Sally took the bus as usual. When she arrived at school, Max Sawyer was waiting in the doorway of their classroom, which looked like a huge living room. He was waiting for Sally and the other children so that he could hear from each one what it was they wanted and needed from him to get started on their projects. Max had been studying about meteorology over the summer and was looking for a group of students to help redesign the school's weather station. Sally volunteered and the school year began.

Dick and Jane Go To College

Once upon a time in a suburb of Detroit, Jane Wilson was packing her suitcases and heading East to attend college. Jane was on her way to Boston University, just across town from Northeastern

University where Dick was a senior. Jane was planning to study psychology, and thought she might someday work in the personnel office of a large corporation. Jane had never been away from home before on her own, so going off to college seemed like a very important step.

Dick had traveled to Boston two weeks earlier. He was planning to live in an apartment that year instead of the school dormitory, and had arrived early to give himself time to set up. He was also feeling somewhat depressed because he and his high school sweetheart, Melissa, had split up over the summer. Dick wanted to date other women for awhile, but he also wanted to see Melissa. Melissa, on the other hand, wanted to get married as soon as they both finished college. She had been very angry when Dick told her about what he wanted to do. They had dated each other some after that discussion, but their relationship had not been the same. Everything had always ended in an argument. Dick had finally decided to break up the relationship.

He found himself in a strange position because he missed Melissa but could not go back to those awful arguments. When he heard that she was dating someone else he felt heartbroken and defeated. Yet he did not want to put himself back into the same old rut they had been in during the summer. Dick did not talk much about Melissa to anyone. He could not think of anyone to talk to about how he felt. When he tried to speak to a couple of his old roommates, they gave him a large bag of marijuana, which he then smoked every day.

Dick planned to pick Jane up at the airport when she arrived, so he left in plenty of time to allow for Boston traffic. When Jane arrived, he was very glad to see her. He called her "squirt," and then put his arm around her and welcomed her to college life. Jane was glad to have a big brother, but felt worried about Dick because she could see from his eyes that things were not going well. She debated whether to ask him about Melissa, and then decided that some things were better left unsaid.

When they arrived at Jane's dorm, students were lined up in the lobby for room assignments. Jane got in line and Dick returned to his apartment. Jane started talking to the students around her. They asked each other where they were from and what their majors would be. Jane was the only psychology major in the group. Regardless of their majors, as freshmen they would all be taking most of the same courses, including Psychology 101, Western History

101, English Literature 101, Philosophy 101, and some mathematics course based on their previous study and current major.

When Jane got to her room she took out her curriculum card. She was surprised to see how similar these subjects seemed to be to the ones she had already taken in high school. She realized that she had very little interest in anything but the psychology course, but decided, again, that this was just the way things were. If she wanted a degree, she would simply have to get through these courses. As Jane was a reasonably good student, she knew she would pass the courses somehow. And she knew there would be plenty of parties and college men to keep her entertained for the next four years.

Dick had returned to his apartment. Two of his roommates, Mike and George, brought out some marijuana and all three began to smoke. Soon they were all laughing about school. Mike was an engineering major like Dick, while George was majoring in chemistry. All three knew they would have a heavy course load this year and were all somewhat worried about the amount of studying that would be required of them.

Mike started laughing. At first he could not control himself, but finally he looked at his friends and said, "Imagine hiring *me*? I can't even fix a broken toilet, but I'm a civil engineer who can build highways." George laughed too, and said that it would not matter because engineers made enough money to hire people to fix their toilets. Dick just grew more silent and depressed. Smoking with his roommates reminded him of the times when he and Melissa would get high, go for long walks, and eat huge ice cream sundaes.

Dick gazed into the light of the lamp. He felt empty inside and wondered why he felt this way. He had always thought that he had so much going for himself. He was bright, good looking, and popular. He had never had to face the failures that others around him seemed to have to face. Yet, in his own way, he felt that he had failed at something, although he was not sure what it was that he had not accomplished.

The school year passed quickly for Jane and Dick. Jane did well but found the required amount of studying a burden. She went to a lot of parties and dated a junior for awhile, something she really liked because it made her feel older. She decided to go to a resort area in the Catskills for the summer and waitress at one of the large hotels. Most of her friends were going and it seemed like it might be fun. Once in a while, she wondered when she would get to the real courses in psychology so that she could learn about people. She always ended up deciding that she would just have to get through the required subjects before she could get to her real interests.

Dick graduated and landed a job with a highway surveying crew for the summer. He decided to wait for the Fall to pursue a job with an engineering firm. He had met a new woman during semester break and they were still going together. Dick had some thoughts of marriage, but wanted to establish himself in a career first. Stephanie, his new love, had also just graduated. She was an English Literature major who was trying to find a teaching job but had so far been unsuccessful.

Ted and Sally Go To College

On Ted and Sally's planet, college began when students were about fifteen years old. Any student who wanted to attend college was required to travel around the planet or throughout the galaxy for three years. In the olden days, most students traveled around their own planet because their help had been very much needed there. Students would go into various impoverished or disaster-stricken areas and help with the problems of homelessness, hunger, and disease. Most college students were moved by these experiences and many returned to the regions where they felt their help was most needed. As a result, Ted and Sally's planet no longer suffered from widespread poverty and unmanageable disease.

In more recent years, many college students from Ted and Sally's planet traveled to Earth to receive their education. They did not go to attend Earth's universities or anything like that. They usually chose Earth because this planet had so many problems that college students could find plenty of places where they could go and help out.

Sally was planning to head to Earth for her first year of school. She had already decided to spend the first six months of college in Addis Ababa, Ethiopia, working with a government project organized to distribute food supplies to the central regions of this nation. Sally had chosen this project because she felt it would help her to work with people. She decided that this project would give her a chance to find out about people from other nations and worlds as well as those college student volunteers from her own planet who had also come to help.

Not all college students went to places like Ethiopia. Some stayed on their own planet to work in government offices, banks or other situations where students who were interested in politics or economics could get some first-hand experience. Regardless of their choice of countries, all students were required to learn the language of any region they chose to visit. During each year they could choose two different areas on the same planet if they could fulfill the language requirements. At the end of each year, students gathered for thirty days to share stories, pictures, and experiences.

There were no grades or performance ratings of any kind. Many of the students involved themselves in service positions. Most students used these experiences to find out where they belonged and how they could fit in on their planet or elsewhere in the galaxy. College was used to help young adults find out more about what they wanted to know in order to function in their choices of environments.

Sally would be traveling with two of her classmates for the first part of the trip. Then she would be on her own. She was looking forward to her journey with excitement and anticipation. Ted had traveled to the region just south of Sally's destination, so he had many helpful suggestions about how to get around in that environment. Ted had already completed his three years of college. During that time, he had decided to return to Barcelona, Spain. There he had found boatbuilders who were using very traditional methods. He had gotten a teaching job in a small boatbuilding school for children. Much of his day had been spent teaching the young ones how to build small dinks and sailboats. In his spare time, he had watched and helped the master boatbuilders, trying to absorb all that they knew.

Ted was living with a woman whom he felt he loved. He found real friendship with her. Elaine, his partner, was seventeen. She and Ted decided to have a child as soon as Elaine could become pregnant. On Ted's planet, couples always had their children in their mid-teens and early twenties when it is most natural for them. In a healed society, this is the age when people have the necessary energy and interest to care for infants and young toddlers. On Ted's planet people were treated and respected like adults throughout their school years, so becoming an adult was no problem.

Elaine was interested in medicine. When she was ready she would be going to medical school for two or three years. She planned to eventually work in a large urban hospital, so half of her student time would be spent in class, and the other half working in the hospital. Elaine would not be taking literature, history, art or any other courses she did not need or find interesting. She would only study those subjects that would help her do what she wanted to do.

Sometimes people on Ted's planet would study a subject such as economics for a year, then apprentice at a large bank or government organization which was actually setting financial policy. After a year or so the student would return for another year of study. This would also often take place in another part of the world since all economists were taught to think in terms of one world economy.

Sally settled into her first year of travel. She found the changes in the environment both interesting and difficult. She was shocked at times to see how poor and undernourished some people were. She wondered how some of them stayed alive. Although her living quarters were quite meager, they were wholesome compared to the lifestyles of the people she worked with each day. The language was difficult to learn at first because the sounds were nothing like Sally's native language and the words were much longer and harder to remember. However, over the months, with the help of the people, Sally learned the language well enough to get her job done.

At the end of the year, Sally was already making plans for her second year of travel. She was considering a job in a government office on another planet, such as being a messenger in the United States Senate. She would have a chance to observe the workings of government in another nation, and she could also volunteer for a social service program for the homeless on weekends. There were many other possibilities at home since Sally's whole planet was open to the college programs. Students were always traveling from one region to another. Most governments had service programs where students could both learn and help out. There were construction projects, medical projects, infant care projects and educational projects where students themselves could teach practical skills in farming, health, and environmental improvement.

By the time students finished their three years, they usually knew more about where and how they wanted to spend their lives. Some returned to areas where they felt they were most needed.

Others began working in business or industry. Some went into medicine and economics, while others pursued crafts and trades. Everyone had a place and each place was valued.

Reader's Test

1. *Which of these four people know more about human relationships?*

   A. Dick and Jane   B. Ted and Sally

2. *Which of these four people are more prepared for parenthood?*

   A. Dick and Jane   B. Ted and Sally

3. *Which of these people would you rather have as neighbors?*

   A. Dick and Jane   B. Ted and Sally

4. *With which of these people would you rather eat lunch?*

   A. Dick and Jane   B. Ted and Sally

5. *Which of these people do you think would be more helpful in a medical emergency or natural disaster?*

   A. Dick and Jane   B. Ted and Sally

6. *Which of these people would you rather have as an immediate supervisor?*

   A. Dick and Jane   B. Ted and Sally

7. *Which of these people would you rather have join your group's project at your company?*

   A. Dick and Jane   B. Ted and Sally

8. *Which of these people have a world view?*

   A. Dick and Jane   B. Ted and Sally

9. *Which of these people are more likely to make a positive contribution to society?*

   A. Dick and Jane   B. Ted and Sally

10. *Which of these people have actually received an education?*

    A. Dick and Jane   B. Ted and Sally

3

THE ORIGINS OF MODERN EDUCATION

NOTE: This is a book about reality. Reality is not positive. Reality is extremely negative.

MODERN EDUCATION IS rooted completely in the human world. To understand its origins, one must first know something about the structure and function of the human world. It is also necessary to know that the human world and the spiritual world are very different. If everything on this planet was functioning in a natural and healthy way, the human world would be an outward, physical manifestation of the inward, nonphysical, spiritual world. It would truly be "on earth as it is in heaven." However, humanity has been living in a long era of darkness so that the human world now reflects only the goals, ideas, and expectations of the human world, without direction from the inner or spiritual world. This means that anything originating from the human world, no matter how well-intended it might be, can only lead to further endarkenment.

When We speak about humanity living in darkness, We are referring to the fact that people have been living without the guidance and direction of the spiritual world. The human world is a world of extreme limitations and misinformation. It is, by its nature, a world in which almost everything is turned backward. When people say one thing, they very often mean the opposite. For example, people who claim to "have an open mind" usually mean that they are closed to any ideas that do not match their own. When people say they only want their enemies to find peace and happiness, they usually mean that they are still hurt and have not forgiven those enemies enough to be able to wish them happiness of any kind.

One of the most blatant examples of the backward nature of the human world is the celebration of Christmas. People call Christmas a joyful holiday. Yet, most people are more depressed and unhappy during the Christmas season than they are at any other time of the year. They do all the human things that make them miserable. They seek excess, excitement, overstimulation, and glamour, all of which lead them into depression and exhaustion. People celebrate Christmas when the sun is in the astrological sign of Capricorn. Any astrologer can verify that this is energetically the least joyful time of the year. Capricorn brings seriousness, hard work, and focus. Sagittarius, on the other hand, would be a much more amenable energy for a holiday celebration if people feel they must have such celebrations.

Most people are aware that Christmas rarely turns out to be a joyful holiday. They know that they feel exhausted and depressed. Some take weeks and even months to recover from this season. Yet, very few people have the resources to stop themselves from participating. In fact, because the human world is so turned around, the more people talk about doing less at Christmas, the more hyped up and commercial Christmas becomes. Ten years ago people complained about seeing Christmas displays before Thanksgiving. Now many stores feature Christmas displays and sales in late September. The more people complain about the commercialization of Christmas, the more commercial it becomes. The complaining only energizes the problem and makes it worse. The human physical world is like a photographic negative. All the black images are white and all the whites are black. The image in the negative is the reverse of reality.

The human world is also a world of polarities. It is a world of good and evil, right and wrong, up and down, in and out, back and forth. It is a world in which people who claim to be doing good are always doing an equal amount of harm, unless their acts of service are a result of some spiritual direction. Since so very few on this planet are spiritually directed, even the most well-meaning people are doing equal amounts of good and evil in the world.

For example, Nancy Reagan has worked very hard at trying to confront drug problems in the United States. She has given of herself, her time, and her energies in ways which for her are quite sincere. Yet, since she started her "Say No" campaign, drug problems and adolescent suicides are on the rise. Her campaign has failed because even though she is trying to do good, her direction comes only from the human world. In her efforts, she has failed to understand that America's drug problems are largely a function of a meaningless and primitive educational system that promotes feelings of personal failure. Most serious drug users can tell you that they feel like failures. Many have, in fact, failed in school. Their drug taking only temporarily alleviates the feelings of failure and uselessness. Very serious drug addicts feel like such useless failures that they think nothing of using other addicts' needles—in spite of the rampant AIDS epidemic—because they see their lives and themselves as having no value.

When Nancy Reagan or a movie star or famous athlete appears on the television screen telling people "not to be pushed" and to "say no to drugs," they are really saying, "Be like me and don't use drugs." If drug users could be famous athletes, first ladies and movie stars, they probably would not care about using drugs because they would not feel like failures. How many women drug users in New York City will ever become the First Lady? How many San Francisco heroin addicts can play basketball like an NBA player? When people who already feel like failures are told by someone who is very successful to "say no to drugs," their feelings of personal failure are only intensified, along with their drug problems. So, although Nancy Reagan wants to do good in the world, she only adds to the drug problem instead of making it better.

The same thing is true for most psychotherapists who began their careers with the idea that they wanted to help people lead more peaceful lives. Despite their intentions, after several years of education and certification, their only impact is to burden their clients with heavy financial payments and incorrect information about how to improve their lives. As a result, most people who attend psychotherapy sessions are in worse shape when they are finished. Their original or "presenting problems" naturally disappear over time. They foolishly credit their therapists with the relief, and then actually end up taking on the therapist's problems along with a large body of psychological misinformation.

The point is that anything originating in the human world is destined to fail, no matter how well-intended and purposeful it may appear to be. Modern education is a product of the human world. It has no basis in reality. Education is based on ideals which are talked about in teacher preparation programs but which, in fact, never actually manifest in reality. Most educators can readily recall learning certain ideological principles in college. Most educators and school officials still agree with these ideals today. However, practical reality in the classroom does not allow teachers to respond to any of the students' real needs or to serve them in any way. The message that educators quickly learn when they enter an educational system is to forget their ideals and conform to the system's standards or be fired.

Educators know they need to relate to the children. They know that children need people who are interested in them and who will talk to them about their interests. Educators know that when children have problems reading, giving them more remedial reading to do makes the situation worse. They know that children have all kinds of things going on in their lives. They know that the average child has ups and downs, loves and hates, fears, angers, and joys; and that they as educators are unable to respond properly to any child.

The message that children get is not that teachers care about them. The message that children get is that teachers do not relate to them. The medium is always the message, as we have already said. The ideal that teachers should relate to students is not enough. The reality that teachers do not relate to children is what children learn.

This is true for almost every aspect of education. Teachers know that students cannot learn about life by sitting in a classroom. Ideally, teachers would like to teach children about life. Showing students pictures about life and having them memorize words about life does not teach them about life. As a result, children only learn the medium and not the idealized message. The medium tells them that nothing in life is real because nothing in the classroom is real. The medium tells them that you do not have to relate to life or people in any way to get along in the world. The real message is that being connected up with reality is not important.

Education does exactly the opposite of what it claims to do. Most parents know this is true in the same way they know that Christmas is not a joyful time of year. But in the human world backward is normal, which is why everything stays the same, even systems that do not work and may hurt people.

Advancement of the Human Mind

One of the key ideas in the structure of the modern educational system is the idea that education improves and advances the human mind. This idea began in the societies of the ancient Greeks and Romans many hundreds of years ago. At that time, several great thinkers were born into the Greek society. These included men like Plato, Socrates, and Aristotle. All of these people came into that culture at a time when people needed to become less physically aggressive and more civilized and cooperative. The ancient Greeks, who were quite barbaric at the time, needed to settle down and shift to a more mental and less physical approach to life. In order to aid in this socialization process, the Brotherhood sent in men like Plato and Socrates who had remarkable mental gifts for that time.

By today's standards the early Greek thinkers would be considered quite average in intellect, because of the gains that have been made in the human mental systems since that time. To credit the current educational system with any of these gains, however, would be a serious error. In many cases, the educational system has actually impeded humanity's mental development.

Plato, Socrates, Aristotle, and others of the ancient Greeks had a specific mission to accomplish in that particular society at that particular time. They came in only to help a few key people in that society shift their focus away from physical aggression. Their followers were only to receive ideas about the human mind and the need to use it, and to receive impressions about the soul which Socrates spoke of throughout his work.

These men were born into Greek society to help calm the barbarism of that society's approach to life, and to create ideas of citizenship and proper value systems. They each described a way that they as individuals could understand life, much in the same way that Einstein mapped out his way of understanding life. None of these men—including Einstein—intended for people to copy what they had each individually proposed. If these men would be able to tell people today about their work from that earlier time, they would each tell people not to try to follow what they did then. They themselves have all progressed on to much greater methods of understanding human existence.

When the ancient Greek thinkers met with their students, they did not mean to lay the groundwork for an educational system that would propose to serve millions of students. They were working with only a handful of young men, most of whom held positions of wealth and power within that society. It was anticipated that these students could potentially influence their countrymen toward a more civilized state of existence.

However, as with the lives of Jesus and Muhammad, humanity completely misinterpreted what Socrates and the others were trying to do. Socrates was not trying to establish an educational system, any more than Jesus was trying to start a religion. Jesus had a specific message that he was attempting to deliver to a specific group of people during that time in history. He was trying to teach people that in order to grow spiritually, one must make many sacrifices. Some of these sacrifices are more difficult than people can possibly imagine. Each individual is required by spiritual law to do his or her own growing and sacrificing.

When Jesus died, his followers and their followers completely misinterpreted his message. Because Jesus lived in a time of darkness, his message fell into the human world where it was immediately reversed. Once people translated his message through the human world, everything he said came out backward. People decided that Jesus sacrificed himself for them. They decided that only Jesus had to make a sacrifice, and that humanity no longer needed to do anything about spiritual growth. People decided that this planet would be a world of personal salvation through religion, rather than a world of spiritual evolution through individual sacrifice.

Jesus did not write the Bible, nor did he read it. He did not instruct anyone to write it, or to proclaim it as a guidebook for spiritual growth. He was crucified, in part, because people did not understand what he was trying to do. By 55 A.D. people arrived at the false conclusion that Jesus had died to save them, and they decided they would document this in stories later compiled as the Bible. Everything Jesus attempted to do was interpreted in reverse by the human world. Although the Brotherhood and the Logos of this planet were aware of the possible distortions concerning Jesus' mission, the distortions that did emerge were the worst of all possible scenarios. As explained in *Modern Religion and the Destruction of Spiritual Capacity*, this idea of personal salvation has set humanity back spiritually in a way that people cannot imagine, because it would be just too devastating.

Like Jesus, Socrates, Plato and Aristotle were trying to impart a specific set of ideas to a particular group of people at a particular time in history. They never intended to provide a model for classrooms centuries later where students sit at the feet of the lecturing teacher. They did not write to have their works memorized—a practice which severely damages the mind—nor did they expect to become primary reading material for every Philosophy 101 course on the planet.

People decided that in order to become like the great thinkers one merely had to study and memorize what the great thinkers had said. Once people came to this false conclusion, all further intellectual development was seriously curtailed. Thinking is not memorizing. One cannot develop the mind by memorizing someone else's ideas just as people could not be spiritually saved by placing their faith in Jesus. Memorizing is not a thinking activity any more than praying to Jesus is a spiritual activity. It is not possible for a person to develop his or her own original ideas by memorizing someone else's ideas. Socrates understood this completely which is why he did not write books for people to memorize. Once people begin to memorize someone else's ideas they destroy that aspect of their own mental vehicles which is actually capable of original thought and imagination.

The early Greek thinkers were attempting to help civilize their society by teaching the idea of good citizenship. They saw that barbaric warfare was depleting people's resources and failing to produce positive results. They were, in a sense, attempting to help curtail the violence in that society.

Ironically, the subsequent misinterpretation of the idea of advancement through education has caused a new kind of violence. It is a mental violence that grows out of the disassociation from reality that is caused by modern education. Education, because it is so disconnected from real life, causes people to construct false realities based on false value systems. The fact that young adults spend more of their energy on makeup and how to dress, rather than on contributions to society is one visible symptom of this false value structure. The kind of glamour and sensationalism that has become the focus of adolescent life is a precursor for violence because it is energetically so removed from the natural course of human life. On the following pages We will discuss the effects of modern education on Western society, the influence of glamour and sensationalism on this planet, and the resulting mental violence that continues to grow as people become more disconnected from reality.

Advancement of Society

Modern education prides itself on being able to produce healthy, contributing citizens. Education implies the improvement of the individual condition and preparation for something to be accomplished in life. People have reached the conclusion that the more educated a society becomes, the more that society can advance in the world. In reality, the more a society advances in education, the more that society loses the relationship between cause and effect. The more educated any society becomes, the more its citizens believe that they and their nation can act with complete impunity.

The ancient Romans modeled their educational system on that of the Greeks. They set up special schools where language, art, and music could be taught. As their society grew increasingly educated, the people became more elitist, gradually losing their connection between cause and effect.

The people of the United States believe that their country is a thriving and flourishing nation. When compared to other less fortunate countries on this planet, this idea of an advancing nation appears to be true. However, upon closer examination one will quickly observe the signs of a declining world power. Since business school graduates—who know nothing about the manufacturing system—have taken over many of the major American companies, the United States has rapidly lost its manufacturing base. These "educated" men and women know nothing about their companies' products, nor do they understand that a manufacturing base is necessary to preserve a capitalist economy. Many unemployed auto and steel industry workers can tell you that there is something very wrong with the American economy.

Modern education teaches people to believe that anyone without a college degree has no value. Welders and steel workers, auto mechanics and assembly line workers, carpenters and mill workers, plumbers and pipe manufacturers, electricians and farmers all have no value. The Industrial Arts Departments are filled with potential dropouts and failures. When no value is placed on the people who are most able to rebuild and restore a society in times of disaster, that society is declining. It is not advancing. Despite all of its high technology, the United States has destroyed its manufacturing system and will soon destroy its farming system, regardless of the fact that farmers are responsible for the nation's food supplies. When a large portion of any society becomes so "educated" that its people can no longer repair the things they need for their very survival, that society is declining.

The Challenger spacecraft accident is an example of what happens when a society and all of its citizens have decided that they can do anything. This accident occurred because Americans have concluded that people can do anything they want to do. People cannot. They need talent. Not every basketball player can join the NBA—only the very best. This fantasy has been the theme behind the space program. It has doomed this program to a series of failures until people can discover, through failure, that there are things they simply cannot do. They cannot launch rockets in cold weather without the proper o-rings. They cannot accomplish anything they decide to do just because they are Americans who try. Certain things require skill and talent. Rocket construction requires extreme skill and expertise, and perfect launch conditions for successful flights.

When the Challenger exploded before America's eyes, people quickly covered up the tragedy with more incorrect and deadly ideas about aiming high and going for the brass ring no matter what. Because everyone covered the Challenger disaster with more of the same worthless assumptions, several more failures were necessary before the American space program officials could even begin to connect cause and effect.

The Voyager excursion is another example of this same thinking. The people who invested in the Voyager invested in an adventure, and once again in the fantasy that people can do anything they set their minds to do. They certainly were not contributing to their nation's improvement, because the Voyager excursion did nothing for the United States. If all those resources had been used to help American farmers, or to provide proper medical care for AIDS patients, the nation would have been improved, and society would be advancing.

Japan is another nation on the decline. The Tokyo stock market is skyrocketing out of control just like the American stock exchange surged upward before the Great Depression. The Japanese people are crazed with financial success. They believe it is completely acceptable to spend forty-million dollars on a painting while a third of the world is hungry.

Young Japanese men and women now spend millions of dollars on makeup each year. Men wear eye makeup, rouge, and face powders just like women. It is disturbing enough to have women make themselves up as a way of imitating real beauty. Women have always found it necessary to attract men's attention by using sexual wiles and snares. This is simply the nature of the female polarity. When men make themselves up, however, they not only substitute glamour for real beauty, but they completely distort the natural uses of the male polarity. Any society that spends millions of dollars on makeup, and disturbs the normal male and female polarities, is not advancing. It is declining into extreme distortion and chaos.

Ironically, the Soviet Union sees itself as a declining society. It is actually a society that is attempting to lift itself up out of a long period of darkness. The Soviet Union has a long way to go before it will begin to value its individual citizens. However, Gorbachev is not buying forty-million dollar paintings while the people of Russia are in need of social and economic uplifting. The Russians are not destroying their farming industry because they are still connected with the fact that farmers grow the food.

A declining nation is one which has lost its calmness and peace. Like the United States and Japan, a declining nation is one which suffers from overstimulation, chaos, and confusion. When the people who live in these countries become aware of the chaos, they try to move away from it. They try to find quiet vacation spots, and begin to move as families or one-by-one to less crowded cities and towns. They try to find calmness along the seashore and in the mountains. Unfortunately, people do not see that they have become the chaos. They are the noise which they are trying to avoid. Many long-time residents of Maine, Vermont, and other once quiet states can tell you that their new residents are polluting the coastlines and the mountains as these immigrants attempt to get away from what they have become.

Americans will know that their society has stopped declining when the physicists stop building nuclear power plants on fault lines. They will know their society has started to advance once again when the people who build the nuclear power plants are prepared to store the nuclear waste products in their own back yards, because they are so certain they have developed proper containment systems. Americans will know that their society has been restored when people become concerned about what is going to happen to America in a hundred years as a result of how they all live today.

Education as Sacred

During early medieval times, education was generally confined to monastic schools which were controlled by the Catholic Church. The monastic schools were established primarily to preserve the literary works of that time from destruction. The early part of the medieval era was a violent and destructive time. People were completely preoccupied with ownership, which is one of the lowest forms of human activity. They wanted to own land, power, and one another. Warfare was a continuous activity.

The Catholic Church wanted to own and preserve all of the previously written works, and the feudal lords wanted to destroy that which they could not own. They thought nothing of attacking a monastery or library and burning everything contained within that structure. The monks, under the leadership of the Catholic Church, were ordered to copy as many books as they could. Very little of what they were copying actually had any real value. However, they spent their days copying books so that the feudal lords and their barbaric armies would not be able to destroy the existing works. Students attending the monastic schools were taught to read and write. Many of them also assisted the monks in the task of copying books and manuscripts which the Catholic Church was attempting to preserve.

Until this time, the wealthier children of most societies had been the educated ones. As previously discussed, educating the wealthy and powerful began with the Greeks and Romans. During the Middle Ages, the poorer classes sought education with the goal of improving their lives and becoming like the rich. They believed that education was definitely inspired by God, but they were also attempting to use education as a means of bridging the enormous gap between the rich and the poor.

This period in history formed many of the basic ideas about education that are still held today by most people in Western society. Because the Catholic Church controlled the monastic schools, people came to believe that education was a sacred and holy thing. And, since the monks were seen as spiritually-inspired teachers, people carried this image forward energetically until they concluded that all teachers, like nuns and priests, were inspired by God.

In reality, during medieval times the Catholic Church was the darkest force on the planet. It is still, today, an endarkened system that destroys anyone who takes it seriously. Its leaders during the Middle Ages were corrupt, unevolved and, in some cases, quite barbaric. They were concerned only in establishing their organization as a world power base. They had no regard for their followers' physical, mental, or spiritual well-being. These leaders were no more inspired than the Catholic hierarchy of today. They were only more violent and overtly corrupt.

To imagine that modern education is a sacred and holy thing because it was once controlled by the Catholic Church is to blind oneself in a way that prevents evaluating and altering the educational system. Once the human consciousness establishes something as sacred, it no longer scrutinizes it or questions its validity. The Catholic Church is still a very dark force on the planet today. It is a product solely of the human world and therefore cannot offer people anything that will promote their spiritual growth, regardless of its claims to be the one, true religion. Yet, no one questions the Catholic Church. No one examines its meaningless, made-up rituals to determine whether those rituals are actually producing spiritual results. No one looks at how this organization spends its financial resources, nor does anyone consider the fact that its very leaders are often psychologically disturbed, depressed men with no ability to relate to others.

Now this same blind acceptance plagues modern education. No one closely scrutinizes the results of this system on people's lives. No one looks at how children feel about going to school, or whether school actually prepares them for life. No one questions the methods of the educational system, which are extremely primitive and often even dangerous. No one really investigates the psychological condition of the system's teachers. In fact, people grant teachers the same kind of protective, societal veil that they grant to ministers, rabbis, nuns and priests. This veil allows teachers to humiliate and abuse children in the name of education, without being held accountable for their destructive behaviors. No one questions whether today's teachers are actually qualified to teach and tend children. Humanity treats education as a sacred and holy institution in the same way that it blindly approaches religion.

We would like to re-emphasize the fact that everything in the human world is completely backward. If the human idea is that something will cause advancement, it will probably cause decline and destruction. If the human idea is that something like religion or education is divinely inspired, it is more likely to be a product of the worst kind of human darkness. It will be many, many years before humanity can comprehend this reality.

Wealth and Success Through Education

During the Middle Ages, people came to the conclusion that education could bridge the gap between the rich and the poor. At that time the rich were very wealthy, while the poor suffered from extreme deprivation. Indeed, the idea of teaching reading, writing, and mathematics to all children was a basically sound idea which did help to bridge the gap between rich and poor. At the same time, however, people also came to the false conclusion that education could make the poor become rich. Today people still hold to this false and destructive conclusion.

The wealthy in medieval times were usually born into their circumstances. Their families, for whatever reasons, had been wealthy for many generations. They were the feudal lords and keepers of the castles. Rarely, if ever, did a young man become wealthy once he was born into poverty. Education may have allowed some young men and women to be lifted out of poverty, because they became more useful to the existing wealthy classes, but poor children did not become rich as a result of education.

In Western societies today people still believe that it is possible to become rich by going to school. People believe that success cannot be achieved in life without a college education. This idea has caused many problems.

People today do not become rich as a result of attending school any more than did the medieval poor. The wealthy people of Western societies have generally been born into wealth. Like the feudal lords, their families have maintained their wealth for generations and live in mansions with servants. Those poor in Western society who do become educated may join the middle class, but this is usually only because they are able to provide some service that is needed by the wealthy, just as in feudal times.

The problem for those who do improve themselves financially because of their education is that they are then motivated by money. They want to become like the rich. They want imitation mansions in the suburbs with hired help, just like the feudal lords. They lose all focus on contributing to the society in which they are living, because education has taught them to place their focus on achieving a life like the wealthy of their society. They rarely achieve the wealth they are aspiring to because most people do not become wealthy as a result of going to school. Yet, instead of doing the spiritual things for the growth of their own souls that they came to this planet to do, they use up their resources trying to imitate the rich.

The more educated a society becomes, the more that society tends to increase its national debt. This is a direct result of people trying to imitate the wealthy, and also losing contact with the reality of cause and effect. The latter will be discussed throughout this book. The former can be seen each day in American spending habits. In their attempts at imitation, people tend to spend beyond their means. Credit cards allow people to pretend they have more financial resources than they actually have. The most educated people tend to have the highest credit lines. They are allowed to borrow whatever money is needed to buy their imitations of wealth. They consider their homes, cars, and wardrobes to be symbols of the success which they have earned through education. But they always strive for more because they are attempting to become rich.

Those men and women who use education to succeed financially in the world are the ones who often have the internal resources and abilities to contribute to society in other ways. They are usually the ones who would be capable of helping the hungry, homeless, and suffering people on the planet. However, their resources are so tied up in attempting to imitate the rich that they have no energy or interest in uplifting the planet. Thanks to modern education, all they can see are their New Age imitation castles in the suburbs, their stock portfolios, and their country club memberships, while the poor and homeless grow in numbers.

Those very few who do become truly wealthy achieve this as a result of their personal inventiveness rather than their education. They become wealthy because they have been able to invent a product or provide a service that people absolutely cannot or will not do without. The product or service must fall into a vacuum or a hole that has not yet been filled. The people who are able to do this are inventors. They are the Thomas Edisons of the society. Edison—one of the world's greatest inventors—had very little formal education, which is why he was able to invent so many different things. Formal education destroys the imaginative and inventive qualities in people because of its "one size fits all" approach, and because education has mistaken memory for intellect. The more educated people become, the more linear and less imaginative they become.

Western societies today are breeding a new generation of flatheads: children who are without imagination and inventive ability. These are the children who started school at two-and-a-half or three years of age so that they could get a head start. Now they are eight and nine years old, and have already spent six or more years in school. They have been studying and memorizing instead of developing their natural skills and abilities. They are completely linear and already demonstrate the same problems of linear living that once could be found in people only after twelve years of education. Soon humanity will have no more Edisons, because they will be destroyed by the time they reach the third grade. It is now less likely that a person will become wealthy as a result of being educated than it was during the Middle Ages, when the idea began. However, humanity has everything turned backward and is, therefore, more convinced than ever that education is the road to power and wealth, and that power and wealth are worthwhile goals.

Today, college is a ticket. People only go to college because they believe that they can get better jobs. They can earn more money and have more power. College has nothing to do with education. It is strictly a matter of economics. It has nothing to do with anyone being trained in anything or being prepared to do anything in the world. It is simply a matter of buying a ticket to more wealth and power.

Everyone knows this is true. Most college students do not even know what they are doing in college besides picking up their ticket to future economic success. What is taught has no relationship to anything in reality. There are very few subjects that people can use in life after spending four years in college. The result is that people spend these four wasteful years only to insure future increased wealth and power. There is currently no other reason for a person to go to college. Anyone who has been there knows this is true. Yet, people continue to pretend that college has something to do with education. This lie only causes college graduates to become even more disconnected from reality and more focused on justifying the fact that they wasted four years of their lives. The way that people cover the lie is with a good salary which everyone expects to earn once they go to college, even though they know nothing about the world.

Taking Notes

Several years ago a California transactional analyst told the following story. She was attempting to teach her students about the limitations of the human mind. The story went like this:

> *Once upon a time a young husband went out to buy a ham. This was soon after the honeymoon, and they were about to share their first ham dinner. He liked the way she cooked it, but as they sat down for dinner he noticed something different. She had cut both ends from the ham, and why would she do that? When he asked her why, she answered, 'My mother always cut off both ends before she cooked a ham.'*
>
> *Then, when he checked with her mother, he learned another interesting thing. Her mother did not have an answer either except that her mother had always cut off both ends of a ham. Fortunately for the curious husband, Grandma was living too and at last came the chance to question her. 'I have been wondering something, Grandma. Why do you cut off both ends of a ham?' 'Oh,' she said, 'that's easy. My pans are all too small for a whole ham.'**

*Charlie W. Shedd

There are many aspects of modern education which are rooted in this same kind of limited thinking. One example is found in high schools and colleges where students spend their days tediously taking notes on subject matter that is already contained in their textbooks. When these students have completed their courses, particularly in history, philosophy, and some sciences, they usually have notebooks that are almost duplicate textbooks.

This practice of copying textbooks in school began with the monastic schools of the medieval era. The fact that these schools were controlled by the Catholic Church, which wanted to own the written works and manuscripts of the day, has already been discussed. Warring armies thought nothing of burning and destroying monasteries and libraries where these works were kept. The monks were ordered to copy texts in order to preserve as many works as possible. The students of the monastery schools also copied manuscripts, again to preserve the works of that time.

It was falsely assumed that these written materials were actually worth copying. No one really questioned the value of what was being copied because people simply assumed that the work of the monks was inspired and therefore was correct. In the same way, it is falsely assumed today that high school and college teachers are saying things and offering lectures that are worth copying. For the most part they are not.

When the monks were copying manuscripts, there were no copy machines. The printing press had not yet been invented. People had no means of duplicating a written work other than tediously copying it by hand. The students and monks did not assume that copying manuscripts was a form of education. However, the monastic school became a model for future educational systems, and the idea of sitting for hours taking notes was inherent in the model.

To imagine millions of high school and college students sitting for hours taking notes, and virtually copying meaningless texts, is extremely ludicrous in a high tech society fully supplied with copy machines. It is as ludicrous as cutting off the ends of a ham two generations later because a grandmother once possessed a very small pan. It is even more ridiculous to assume that taking notes and copying textbooks produces any kind of learning. The monks did not learn anything from their endeavors, but they were not trying to learn in this way. They were trying to preserve the manuscripts. Students today do not learn anything from taking notes either. And there are no barbarians coming to burn the schools and libraries. If they did, there would be plenty of copy machines to duplicate anything that was lost, assuming that what was lost would be even worth copying.

Like the young woman who automatically trimmed the ends of the ham because her grandmother did it, modern education still automatically demands that its students copy texts. Like the young woman, no one questions where the practice originated, or why it is being done. It is simply continued blindly, without purpose or meaning, because a long time ago a grandmother had a very small pan.

The Industrial Revolution: The Making Of The Perfect Student

The Industrial Revolution brought another era of great change. Most Western societies rapidly abandoned their agricultural economy in favor of a manufacturing base. People moved away from country living to establish towns and cities around the factories that promised them employment.

It rapidly became clear to Western societies that the nation with the strongest manufacturing base would become the most powerful nation in the world. The nation that could supply the world with manufactured goods would be the most influential in all economic and political affairs. Western nations began competing with one another in the manufacturing of much needed supplies. England, France, Belgium, and Germany all competed for first place.

After the Civil War, the United States capitalized on the energy of opposition that had caused the war, and joined North and South to become the most powerful manufacturing country of all. In order to achieve and maintain this position, the United States, as well as other industrialized Western societies, needed competent factory workers. The manufacturing industry needed people who could perform the same job on the assembly line all day long, with a minimum of error. The factories needed workers who were trained to not make mistakes and to fear the authority of their managers.

Everything in these Western nations was geared toward developing a strong industrial economy—including the public school system. Schools became places where children were prepared for factory life. Teachers became more like factory managers, disciplining their students for making mistakes. Children were tested, graded, and penalized more frequently in an attempt to support the growing industrial economy. Students were punished and humiliated when they made mistakes, so that they would avoid error while working on the assembly lines. Ironically, they were not allowed to take the time to accomplish any kind of real perfection.

Today, American schools are still trying to produce perfect factory workers, even though the nation is quickly destroying its manufacturing base. The methods used during the Industrial Revolution did not yield any of the anticipated results. As a matter of fact, this approach to education only created more hostility between students and teachers which was reflected in the relationships between labor and management. These problems grow continuously more difficult under the influence of education as it exists today.

Schools failed to produce perfect factory workers, because people do not learn by trying to avoid error. In reality, people always learn through error. Attempting to teach students to avoid error caused the educational system to become even more dangerous and endarkened. When people use their resources to avoid error and punishment, learning becomes impossible.

Because factory work required memory and not intellect, humanity substituted memory for intellect during this time. People needed to memorize their assembly line jobs and repeat them over and over without error. Students began to memorize everything, and then they were tested and graded. The legacy of the Industrial Revolution has been the substitution of a good memory for a good mind, and the promotion of a system in which children can no longer learn.

The Industrial Revolution not only required people who were afraid to make mistakes, it also needed cheap, unskilled labor. Education insured this cheap labor force by keeping women away from the industrial arts courses. Taking these courses might have led to the development of real skills for many women. Female students in most school systems today still encounter great resistance when they attempt to take industrial arts courses. Women are also kept away from industrial arts because of their natural skills, and their abilities to pay attention to detail—which far exceed most men's abilities to observe detail. The computer chip industry is a testimony to this fact.

The Industrial Revolution needed factory rats. Mills needed

mindless factory workers who would have no interest in inventing or creating anything and who could run a machine all day without complaining. The people who owned and managed the factories needed a training program. Schools were perfect. The people who worked in the factories paid taxes so that schools could train their children to become future factory workers.

The goals and objectives behind this system were not honorable. There was nothing humanitarian in this approach. This system grew out of a monstrous period in history. These approaches to people are still alive today which is why workers must still be protected by labor unions.

The factory owners of that time were people who wanted to strip the children of their natural abilities early in life and then continue to abuse them later. When the factory owners felt enough guilt for dehumanizing and abusing people, they appeased their guilt by building a library, hospital or an orphanage for the people they had misused. Even in the 1980s, factory owners are still making their contributions to community and school library funds.

Today, schools still function for the industrial revolution. There are no courses in high schools or colleges that teach the potential industrialist how to build safe and decent factories, or how to treat workers properly. There are no courses that teach principles of brotherhood or sharing. There is no information given to future managers and business owners about providing decent wages or insurance benefits to their employees, or about making sure people are cared for when they are sick. And this is why labor and management still face all the same problems they had in the nineteenth century.

Education has developed its own system of manufacturing. Schools have become factories where each student is treated the same, as though children did not have individual needs and singular interests. Educators believe they can turn children on like little computers in the morning and put anything into those little computers that they want to deposit. All children in a particular classroom arc given reading lessons at 9:00 A.M. regardless of how each child thinks or feels, or what each child needs. Every student must learn math at 10:00 A.M., no matter what natural interests they each may have.

A Fullerton, California study indicated that the major discipline problems found in children in the 1940s were ranked as follows:

1. *Talking*
2. *Chewing gum*
3. *Making noise*
4. *Running in the hallways*
5. *Getting out of place in line*
6. *Wearing improper clothes*
7. *Not putting paper in wastebaskets*

These "discipline problems" are all natural responses for children who are being forced to conform to an unhealthy system. Unfortunately, unlike the factory workers of the early twentieth century, the children of the 1940s were too young to form unions and to small to fight back.

That same Fullerton, California study went on to list and compare the major discipline problems found in schools in the 1980s. The list reads as follows:

1. *Drug and alcohol abuse*   6. *Assault*
2. *Pregnancy*   7. *Burglary*
3. *Suicide*   8. *Arson*
4. *Rape*   9. *Bombings*
5. *Robbery*

One would think that such a study might teach educators something about what happens to children when all their natural responses to a disturbed system are successfully stamped out. But, this has not been the case. Educators have concluded, instead, that what children need is more discipline. This increasingly violent behavior has only caused most educators to think they must now "get tough" with children who demonstrate any unwillingness to conform to the manufacturing of "successful" students. Imagine how a list of discipline problems might read for the year 2010.

Educators' Ideas About Children

Modern education is built on the idea that children between the ages of five and eighteen have no natural interest in learning anything, nor do they have any natural desires to contribute to the world. Based on these premises, it therefore becomes the duty of the educational system to devise a structure in which children can be forced to learn, or to suffer the consequences of humiliation and punishment. The educational system assumes that children have no natural interests in life which they could cultivate on their own. It assumes that children will not learn anything unless they are herded into classrooms and forced to memorize information, whether they need it or not.

Religions operate the same way. Religions assume that people have no natural interests in spiritual growth. It is therefore the duty of religious leaders to herd people into churches and synagogues each week and force them under pain of sin to pay homage to God. Religions actually have had a role in society. Their job has been to keep the idea of God alive in people, especially during times of darkness. However, religious leaders have always assumed that people have no natural interests in spiritual growth or in the idea of God. They have concluded that they must use fear and guilt to frighten people into spiritual growth, and into preserving the idea of God.

As a result, no one grows spiritually by participating in a religion. In fact, religions destroy people's natural interests in spiritual growth by engaging them in salvation fantasies that cannot lead them anywhere. Once religion hooks someone on the idea that he or she has been saved, that person loses all interest and motivation in real growth. This occurs because religions convince people that if they simply believe in salvation they need do nothing to improve their own lives or the lives of the people around them. Spiritual growth is actually a process of continuous improvement. People completely abandon this continuous process once they are frightened into accepting the fantasy of salvation.

Educators and school officials approach students with the same kinds of threats and punishments. Educators, like ministers, have very low ideas about humanity. They believe that human beings are lazy, unmotivated, and disinterested in life. If they had higher ideas, educators would see that children naturally want to learn. In a healthy society, education would first provide children with the experiences they need to discover everything they can about themselves and how they work inside—how they feel, how they think, and how others perceive them. Secondly, education would function to help children understand as much about how the world works as would be humanly possible.

Most children are capable of discovering what they need to know about themselves through their relationships with other children. Through interacting with other children, they find out who they are, what they are, and how they fit into their world. Children between five and eight years of age naturally want to accomplish this task. However, when children go to school, they are forced to sit in classrooms where relating and interacting are forbidden. When children do try to interact they are scolded and, in some cases, punished. The healthier children who insist on interacting are labeled as discipline problems and treated as misfits and failures for their efforts.

The second job of any school system in a healthy society would be to prepare children for adult life by teaching them about how the world actually works. This book is about how schools have completely failed to help children accomplish this goal. It simply is not possible to help children discover life by containing them in classrooms, showing them pictures about life, and attaching words to those pictures. You cannot teach children about the world by showing them a map. When children try to learn about life from looking at pictures and memorizing words, they quickly conclude that life is flat, boring and meaningless. These flat, linear approaches to teaching cause children to be drained of their resources at a time in their lives when they are desperate to be enlivened and enriched by direct experiences.

Educators call direct life experiences "field trips." This means that in order to have a direct experience of life, children must leave the classroom and go out into the "field." This approach assumes that what is going on in the classroom is more valuable than what is going on in the world. It also teaches children to think that what they are learning from pictures and words is more valuable than real life. If education were functioning properly, classrooms would be an integral part of life. There would be no difference between experiences in the classroom and experiences in the world, because it would all be real life. Students would not need to be sent out on field trips twice a year, because schools would be an integral part of community life. Schools might provide some central gathering place, but learning would be accomplished everywhere according to each student's special interests.

When educators concluded that children have no natural interest in learning, they also concluded that they as educators must motivate children to learn. Therefore, they never feel the need to look at the fact that what they are teaching is useless and boring. Nor do they recognize and admit that they are only offering education to the few students with good memories, and not to anyone else.

Educators, like ministers, assume that the way to motivate students is through fear and guilt. Students are forced to memorize subjects which have no meaning, and then to take tests on how much they can remember. The testing and grading system is built on the bell-shaped curve. This system insures that some students will do well, some average, and some will fail. If all students do well on a test, the exam is considered invalid and the teacher is thought to be too lenient.

By using the bell curve, educators can support their basic idea that if children are not forced to learn they will idle away their lives doing nothing with themselves. The bell curve insures that only a handful of students will do very well. The rest of the students will either need improvement or they will fail. This system is completely rigged to support educators' low ideas of humanity. It also produces students who eventually become lazy, unmotivated, and disinterested in life because education does not offer them any real opportunities for learning.

Because educators assume that children have no natural interest in learning, and will only learn through coercion, they construct systems in which children are forced to do things they dislike doing. Most school children actually spend all day working on things they hate. They could learn much more by doing things they enjoy each day, but educators have such low opinions and ideas about children that this would never occur to them. Children love to make things and do things with their hands. Most children naturally love electronics, carpentry, boatbuilding, photography, and plumbing—much of which they can readily use in everyday life. Instead, educators offer children subjects which they naturally dislike and cannot use in their lives. Reading, writing and certain forms of mathematics are useful for all children, but even these subjects could be taught in reference to projects which children would find satisfying.

Once children become programmed into spending their days doing tasks they dislike, that program remains with them throughout their lives. Educated adults spend the major portion of their lives attending to work they would rather not be doing. Most people wait until their "retirement" to pursue what they really like, and by that time they no longer know what they enjoy or they are too old and tired to do it.

The modern world is now governed by negative ideas from educators, such as the erroneous idea that people have no natural interest in learning and must therefore be threatened and forced to learn things which they generally abhor. What is so sacred about forcing children to spend twelve or more years of their lives doing things they hate to do? And exactly how do educators then expect those children to grow up and become healthy, contributing members of any society?

Note to the Teachers

Imagine that you are in a room with ninety-nine other teachers. You are sitting in your chair, and you have been asked to participate in a game. The game will last for two hours. The game requires that you take certain quizzes and tests, but the winners receive valuable, useful prizes. You must remain silent during the game and you cannot discuss what is happening with the people around you. If you need to get up to go to the bathroom, you must raise your hand, state the nature of your request, and obtain a pass before leaving the room.

The game begins and everyone hopes they will succeed and win a prize. However, the game is rigged. Only five people out of the hundred can actually win. Everyone keeps trying but the same five people keep winning no matter how hard anyone else tries to succeed. Soon you and the people around you become restless. Everyone starts to wiggle around in their chairs and talk to one another. When they do, the seminar instructors come over and yell at them and embarrass them. Some teachers are even told that they must stay an extra hour after the game to see if they can learn to discipline themselves.

Now multiply this two-hour game by three, and imagine playing in it for six hours. Then multiply the six hours by five days a week. Then multiply the five days a week by forty or more weeks a year. Now, Teachers, you know what it is like to sit in your classrooms.

4

HOW, WHEN & WHY PEOPLE LEARN

NOTE: This is a book about reality. Reality is not positive. Reality is extremely negative.

SEVERAL DECADES AGO, guided and inspired by the Brotherhood, A. S. Neill began an educational experience called Summerhill. The school was considered to be the most unusual and radical school in the world. Neill ran the school for forty years. In his system, children only learned what they wanted to learn, and only when they felt inspired or inclined to do so. Children were taught to govern and discipline themselves and to experience school as something that belonged to them rather than to educators and school officials.

Over time, A. S. Neill was able to clearly demonstrate that when children are left to their own natural devices they will not only seek to learn, but in many cases will do so with a passion. Neill also demonstrated that children need time to discover themselves and their own natural interests, without outside interference from parents and teachers. He further demonstrated that when children are given this time, in an environment with truly supportive adults, those children will blossom into very successful, productive human beings.

People who visited Summerhill knew that A. S. Neill was on to something very positive. Visiting educators and school officials could clearly see a vitality, maturity, and well-being in many Summerhill students, which could not be found in students of more traditional schools.

Most Summerhill graduates went on to live very productive lives. As a group, they did not become successful in the stock market, nor did they all become doctors, lawyers, and politicians. Their standards of personal success had much more to do with leading satisfying, productive lives than with making a lot of money, which is part of the reason why Summerhill was not widely accepted.

Summerhill was obviously a successful project. A. S. Neill's book about this project is still required reading in most educational psychology or child development courses today. People still talk about how much the Summerhill students seemed to learn about themselves, and how they entered adulthood so much more prepared for life than their peers. Yet, this project did not become a model for modern education. In fact, modern education has since become more rigid and less useful, even though all evidence clearly demonstrates that education as it exists has failed humanity. One only needs to ask a class of graduating seniors about their feelings on how their education has prepared them to cope with adult life. Many are so destroyed that they have been rendered incapable of answering the question. Many are still so buried in their own immaturity they do not even know that society expects them to act like adults.

Summerhill was a good idea which was swallowed up by an endarkened system. It was not a perfect educational system, nor is it being offered here as a panacea for all of education's problems. It was an inspired model of how children can learn when they are placed in a reasonably supportive system. Its failure to inspire educators and school officials today is only a symptom of how endarkened education has become.

Children almost always learn about the function of something before they learn about its structure. For example, if an educator wanted to teach children about wrenches in a way that would cause real learning, he or she would find some way that wrenches could be put to practical use in the students' lives. Imagine, for instance, that several children in the class have been complaining about their chairs being loose and unbalanced. The chairs are constructed with metal rods and have wooden seats and backs. The chairs are unstable because several of the nuts at the rod joints have loosened over the years and need to be tightened.

The teacher would give the children a box of wrenches of all sizes and of slightly different construction. The children would then locate the proper size wrench to repair their own chairs. Very quickly, the children would discover that only a half-inch wrench will fit on the loose nuts. They would then tighten the loose nuts and discover that their chairs are once again stable.

Education approaches learning in reverse. Children are expected to read about wrenches in books. If they are lucky, they might see a picture of a wrench. They are never allowed to use or touch a wrench. After reading about wrenches in a book, children are then forced to take a test on what they have read. They are then graded on how much they can remember about wrenches, even though they have never learned to use one. In a very short time, they forget about what they have read. When any real repair job arises that would require a wrench, they have no idea how to use one.

It is impossible to teach children how to function in the real world without letting them learn how the world functions. Studying the structure of something first, without every studying the function, destroys a child's natural ability to learn how to function.

There are a few exceptions. A small number of children can learn by studying something first. They are the ones who need to study first as a way of preparing themselves for actually discovering the function of something. Studying the structure first helps them to avoid being overwhelmed by the function. These students are the ones who need to read the repair manual carefully before opening up the hood of a car.

Even these students must, however, get to the point of discovering how something functions. They must be able to open up the hood of a car and find out how the car works. Educators think children can learn about cars by memorizing the repair manual and never laying their hands on a car.

Protecting the Fantasy

Human begings always learn through failure. People must be able to discover how things work by first discovering something about how they do not work. There is no other way for the human consciousness to acquire real learning.

In order to learn, people must also have contact with the real physical world, not the mental world of books and ideas. They must have the opportunity to make things and build things, and to see the results of their work on a daily basis. They must be able to see how parts of things fit together, and how they do not. They must be shown how to alter parts to make them fit, and to see how certain parts work together—like the parts of a car engine or the parts of a chair.

Over the past two thousand years, humanity has been moving further away from real learning. Schools are now offering more subjects to memorize with the mind and less subjects that involve building or making things. This movement away from reality has to do with humanity's religious ideas and how they have spread.

Right after Jesus died, people decided that they did not need to do anything about their own spiritual growth because Jesus had done it all for them. This meant that people no longer had to be responsible for their lives because they would automatically go to heaven as long as they believed in Jesus. With this incorrect idea implanted, people are free to abuse their children, gossip about their neighbors, cheat on their spouses, steal from their companies, and deceive their friends. Even those people who are not involved in a religion today still carry the influence of these incorrect assumptions throughout their lives.

In reality, this is just a made-up human fantasy. However, people have a lot of energy and resources tied up in this fantasy because they think it prevents them from being in pain. They cannot see that the fantasy causes them pain because it keeps them from actually cleaning up their lives in a way that would bring them much greater peace and satisfaction. When they invest in this fantasy, people think that it helps them not to be so frightened of death. Yet, this fantasy only produces more fear. It causes more fear because it keeps people focused away from the reality of individual spiritual evolution, and prevents them from accomplishing what they came into this lifetime to do. Souls who are accomplishing what they have come to do never fear death the way that people fear it who have wasted their lives on religious fantasies. People fear death mostly because they have not found real satisfaction in life.

To protect their religious fantasies, humanity must avoid reality.

People must avoid finding out how the world works and how it does not work, otherwise they will expose this religious nonsense for what it is. They must prevent one another from building things and making things and discovering how parts fit together.

Modern education is structured to protect the religious fantasy of personal salvation. It is structured in a way that prevents people from being able to learn about reality, so that no one will expose the made-up fantasy. As a result, any attempt to promote real learning will be stamped out by school officials. Any teachers who are genuinely interested in the well-being of children will not survive in the educational system. These teachers will be blocked and obstructed at every turn. Any method or course of study within the system that provides real learning will be eliminated or reserved for students who are too damaged to reap its benefits.

Modern education refuses to allow children to fail in a way that would help them learn. It prevents children from learning by punishing them for their mistakes. Children then learn to focus their resources on avoiding failure instead of using their failures to discover how something actually works.

Imagine a four-year-old child who is learning to build with blocks. If she can build long enough and without interference she can continuously discover reality. Each time her building falls over, she finds out something else about what works and what does not work in the physical world. When she builds too high without a firm foundation, the building falls. When she sets the blocks up without some balance or symmetry, the building falls. Over and over again she fails, but each time she discovers something about how the world works.

Children and adults need to spend their lives finding out how the world works just like the four-year-old girl. Imagine what would happen to the little girl if someone punished her or humiliated her whenever the blocks fell over. Imagine what she would have to do inside of herself to tolerate the punishment and humiliation. Imagine how much energy she would spend trying to avoid making an error. Imagine how much longer it would take for her to learn about the world through her blocks—if she would be able to learn at all.

This is the tragedy that takes place every day in classrooms all over the world. Millions and millions of children and educated adults have all their resources tied up in avoiding error because they do not want to be punished and humiliated again. They are too devastated to be concerned about evolution or learning. They are so fearful of failure that they can no longer grow or learn. Modern education has almost completely stopped all real learning, but it has preserved the fantasy of personal salvation so that people can go on pretending they have been saved.

Cause and Effect

People learn about reality by being able to establish the proper connections between cause and effect. People establish cause and effect by learning about how the world works. For example, people learn not to touch hot stoves usually by touching a hot stove. Cause and effect, in this instance, is established immediately unless a person is suffering from some brain dysfunction. The physical world is a world of cause and effect in which many thousands of such connections must be made for a person to be able to grow.

Modern education uses grades and other forms of punishment to interfere in the establishment of cause and effect. For instance, imagine again the four-year-old girl who is building with blocks. When the building initially topples over, the little girl is beginning to establish cause and effect. At first she might not be able to figure out why her buildings are falling. Eventually, however, she begins to see that there is a consistent cause of the structure's fall. She may discover that no matter how many times she tries to stack the blocks up twenty-five high, they always fall over when she places the last block on the pile. Over the course of weeks, she discovers many reasons why her buildings fall. Each time she does so, she is establishing an internal connection between cause and effect.

However, if she was punished and humiliated every time the blocks fell over, in the way that school systems punish and humiliate children, she would soon be too preoccupied with avoiding failure to make the connections between cause and effect. Her linear mind would take over and she would try to memorize what worked and what did not work instead of being able to learn through direct experience. She would try to memorize what buildings worked, and would avoid anything she feared would not work. Her world of blocks would become more and more limited.

Over the years, modern education has designed a perfect system for destroying cause and effect in the human consciousness. Educators discovered that they could interrupt the establishment of cause and effect by introducing humiliation and punishment. People must defend against the hurt of humiliation and punishment. They do this by moving out of that part of themselves that can learn through direct experience, and moving into their minds. It is simply too painful for people to be open in the way that learning through direct experience would require, when what they would actually be experiencing is hurt and punishment.

Once educators discovered how to prevent the establishment of cause and effect by closing down a person's ability to learn through direct experience, they then began to substitute memory for intelligence. They found that they could further disassociate children from reality by forcing them to use their minds to memorize information that has no meaning. Education teaches people to believe that they can learn about life by memorizing facts from books.

People have no idea how dangerous it is to try to live from memory rather than reality. Memorized facts remain stationary in the human mind. Reality is always changing. What children memorized about the geography of the United States twenty years ago is not reality today. Memorizing facts about electricity from a science book will not teach people anything about how to change a fuse, wire a circuit, or avoid a shock. Memorizing facts about corporate structures has nothing to do with the reality of running a company.

This kind of thinking allows people to believe that one could learn about hot stoves by memorizing the fact that hot stoves burn fingers. This thinking means that people are free to build nuclear power plants and other devices if they can memorize what will happen when the devices explode or the power plants have accidents. It means that people are free to fill the oceans with nuclear waste packaged in leaky, inadequate containers as long as they can calculate and memorize the effects of the nuclear discharge on ocean life.

Once cause and effect is severed, re-establishing its proper relationship is a difficult and painful process. It takes people a long time and many failures to reconnect with reality. The Chernobyl accident has taught humanity nothing, in spite of the lives lost and the destruction to this planet. Thanks to modern education, humanity will need many more Chernobyls and many other tragedies before people can rediscover reality through cause and effect.

Hunger to Learn

Learning always takes place when a vacuum exists in the human consciousness. Simply stated, people only really learn when there is something that they want to know. When they do not want or need to know about something, they have no space or room in the consciousness for that data.

Schools try to force children to take in too much information too fast. Students never have a chance to discover whether or not they need that information. Subjects are thrown at students like a medicine ball. Students then try to take it in all at once.

Life does not come at people all at once. Yet many adults experience life that way. Many educated adults take in much more data than they need every day. They are easily overwhelmed by simple problems because they cannot separate out what needs to be solved from all of the other incoming data.

Summerhill was a Brotherhood-inspired school which was structured to help students discover what they wanted or needed to learn. Students only took courses that they were interested in taking. No one was ever forced to attend class. Each student was completely free to establish his or her own curriculum and to either abide by these schedules or not. No one ever chased them to find out where they were or why they were not in class.

At first, many of the new students at Summerhill who had previously been attending public school refused to attend any classes at all. In the entire history of the school, however, all but one student eventually began to take some courses. And even that child, as an adult, proceeded to run his own successful business. A very high proportion of Summerhill graduates went on to live very successful, relevant lives.

Today, modern education refuses to allow children to build up a vacuum or a need to learn anything. Children between six and eight years of age, if left to explore the world without interference, are like fertile farmlands waiting to be seeded. They are hungry to be with adults who can help them plant the kinds of seeds inside of themselves that will one day blossom into healthy, grown-up lives. This is the time when a child's creativity and imagination are flourishing. It is a time to discover things, invent things, and to manipulate the physical world.

It is also a time for young children to discover what they need and want to know about life. During these years, children are supposed to discover that they can use reading, writing, and math to get along in the world. They should not be locked up in classrooms, trying to memorize words that have no meaning. They should not be stuffed with irrelevant information long before they are ready to learn.

Children between the ages of eight and ten want and need to build things. Most boys and girls in this age range like such things as model airplanes. Imagine what it would be like to have a group of ten students who loved to build model airplanes. Instead of forcing these children to read books which do not interest them or to do math that has no meaning in their lives, imagine what it would be like to teach children aeronautical engineering through the construction of their own aeronautical models. These children would be much more interested in learning to read if they could read about how to improve their own airplanes. They would have far greater interest in math and physics if they could learn how to construct faster, better flying planes through the use of angles and mathematical computations.

Children between ten and twelve often have a natural interest in electronics. Imagine the heightened increase in reading that a group of ten such students would experience if they were reading about how to build their own radios, transmitters and amplifiers. Imagine how their interest in math would increase if they needed to use mathematical formulas to combine the right electrical components on a circuit board so they could make their own walkie-talkies or burglar alarms. Imagine how their understanding of "science" would compare with a group of students who studied about electricity in science books for a semester.

The idea of delaying the teaching of reading, writing, math, and other subjects will be appalling to most parents. Educated parents, especially, want their children to get an early start on these subjects. They want their children to begin to read and write in preschool. These parents have no idea how this approach to education hurts and destroys their young children.

This idea of getting children started early emerged in a popular form in the 1960s. At that time, the United States government began a preschool program called Head Start. The Head Start Project was designed to help socially and economically disadvantaged children prepare for school experiences by filling in some cultural gaps so that the disadvantaged children would be on an equal level with children of more fortunate parents. The program was helpful only in that it removed these children from their chaotic home lives for some portion of the day. It was built on the false assumption that poverty breeds psychological and emotional problems. This is a false assumption because it assumes that middle class families are less disturbed, when in reality middle class families only have their disturbances disguised in more acceptable coverings.

When middle class and upper middle class parents realized that their youngsters might no longer be able to dominate the disadvantaged children, they began to press for their own kind of "head start" programs. They reacted by establishing swim classes for babies, exercise and play classes for toddlers (as if toddlers did not know how to exercise and play without instruction), and very early learning programs to insure that their children could maintain a competitive edge.

Most parents who seek such programs are the same people who competed successfully within the educational system. They are the same people who view education as a road to financial success; even as a means to becoming wealthy. They want their children to do what they themselves have failed to accomplish—which is to become wealthy.

Again, these parents are the ones who have the inner resources to do something about the pain and suffering on this planet. Instead they are consumed with their fantasy that education makes people rich if they only work hard enough. These parents have concluded that the only reason they are not wealthy themselves is that they were not industrious enough. They have also decided that they will push their children to work harder than they did so their children can become wealthy, and thereby fulfill their parents' unrealistic and destructive dreams of personal wealth.

Education has taught these parents to step on anyone in order to reach the top. Their fantasies blind them to the reality of the fact that they are destroying their children's natural instincts and abilities to learn. These parents actually have no idea of the seriousness of this form of destruction. If they knew or could see what was happening to their sons and daughters as a result of their early education programs, ninety-nine percent of these parents would stop. The last one percent would continue but only because of their own inner disturbances.

Children need their parents to provide them with love, food and shelter, tenderness and care. When parents make intellectual demands on their children, parents prey upon the vulnerabilities and needs of the children. The children must make every attempt to please their parents because any loss of approval in the early years is perceived by the children as life threatening.

Educators and psychologists who advocate early education programs do not know anything about children. These "experts," like ministers and priests, have very low opinions of people. They prey upon parents' fears of failing as parents, and promise them that their forms of early training will lead to the development of "superkids." In reality, of course, these experts lead parents into failing their children in some of the cruelest possible ways.

Parents of the 1970s and 80s also have the idea that good parents entertain their children. So instead of allowing children to discover life and who they are as people, these parents fill their children up with television, movies, summer camp, gymnastics, little league, ballet lessons, karate lessons, arts and crafts, video games, toys, and computers. Their children are so filled with mental junk that they have no room to learn about reality. Between parents and teachers, today's children have no vacuums. They have no room to learn. They have no space to develop inventions or to discover life.

When children are fed so much useless data, life becomes both overwhelming and confusing. To the young child, each piece of unnecessary data is like getting a birthday gift that he or she cannot use. Imagine how children feel inside with all those birthday gifts that cannot be used.

In the process of being fed mental junk, children not only get too filled up to be able to learn, but they also get addicted to excitement and stimulation. They grow up without any tolerance for inner peace or calm. They cannot stand boredom, which is often the precursor of creativity. They seek drugs, sex, glamour, and other forms of excitement to keep themselves constantly full. They lose all contact with who they are or what they want because they are too full of mental junk to be able to find out.

This kind of thinking causes educators to do all the wrong things when children have problems learning. When a child is having problems reading, educators try to solve this by giving the child more reading to do. When these children are given remedial reading assignments, the problem usually gets worse. The reason that these children get worse is that education is an assault on their unique way of learning. What most of these children need is a vacation from school, which is the last thing their teachers would ever recommend.

In this system, children have to become hurt in order to learn. They have to conform to a disturbed system even though that system is destructive to them. The vulnerable ones simply cannot conform. The system then tries even harder to force itself on the vulnerable children who, in the end, become severely wounded by the system itself.

Educators know this is true. They know it clearly but they ignore it for political reasons. They know that their curriculums are irrelevant and dangerously inadequate, but everyone wants to keep up the front. No one wants to be fired. People who complain are perceived as radicals at best, and at worst they are considered deranged.

Tension

In order for learning to take place, there is a tension that is necessary. Healthy tension occurs in people when they are strongly motivated from inside themselves to learn something. It is like a hunger and a need to know. Children do not belong in school before age eight, at least as schools exist now. They belong out playing. Many adults today are still trying to sow "wild oats" because they did not play enough when it was natural for them to play.

At Summerhill, teachers did not teach students until they were very hungry to learn. Some teachers at Summerhill would even refuse to work with certain students who, for one reason or another, had not had time to build up the tension necessary to learn. Students had to have some idea what they wanted to learn and why they wanted to learn it before starting a project. Most high school students today have no idea about what they want to learn, or why they would want to learn anything.

Healthy tension also grows from a need to do a good job at something. This assumes that a student is actually doing something that is worth doing well. In most instances, students of modern education have no interest in what they are doing, nor is the subject inherently useful enough for a student to want to do it well.

Healthy tension can often be found in cabinetmakers and boatbuilders, and in people who are making and doing things that yield a positive result in the physical world. Modern education does not provide students with such opportunities. The few industrial arts courses that are available in high schools are usually reserved for potential school dropouts and failures. By the time they arrive in the Industrial Arts Department, these students feel too bad about themselves to be positive about the results of their work. The mediocre and meaningless Arts and Crafts Departments also fail to establish the necessary tension for students to want to produce good results.

Since education systematically prevents the establishment of any healthy forms of tension, it must simulate tension in unhealthy ways just to keep the attention of the students. Education's forms of unhealthy tension do not produce real learning, but they do allow teachers to maintain control over most students. Modern education creates tension through the use of fear and punishment. It motivates students by causing them to use their resources to avoid hurt. The tension that results is a function of fear and worry. It has nothing to do with stimulating natural interest in students.

Over time, this kind of tension produces emotional and mental instability, as evidenced by the growing rate of mental health problems in Western societies. It also promotes the use of certain drugs and alcohol in an attempt to quiet down the tension. Many junior high and high school students who use drugs or alcohol are trying to find emotional relief from the anxiety, worry, and feelings of personal failure that have been inflicted upon them by modern education.

Inspiration and Motivation

For centuries, education has attempted to motivate students through fear and punishment. Students are expected to memorize a certain amount of material, and to remember that material long enough to pass a test. The tests are then graded, and the students with the best memories are given the highest grades. The grades are then presented to students and their parents as if these grades represented some measurement of learning. As a result of seeing their grades, the students are then supposed to be motivated to learn and study harder.

Since modern education is based on memory rather than learning, and data rather than knowledge, this system consistently fails to motivate students. There is nothing for them to learn. There are only subjects to be memorized. Students either have good memories or they do not. Those who have the memories receive higher grades, and those who do not get lower grades.

When this system fails to motivate the students who have the lower grades and poor memories—as it always does—educators and school officials begin to threaten and punish those students. The educators expel them from class, suspend them from school, burden them with more material to memorize, and use any other punishment they can devise. When these punishments fail, the school officials and educators then call in the parents so that everyone can combine forces against the student and inflict more punishment. The fact that this system has consistently failed to motivate students has not deterred educators and school officials in the least. In fact, the more the system fails, the more punishment they inflict on the students.

The system itself is so airtight that no one calls it into question. Parents and teachers simply combine forces and conclude that there is something wrong with the child. No one looks at the fact that the system itself is based only on memory skills, which have nothing to do with intellect. The fact that someone can remember something is not an indication that the person has learned anything. Human minds were not designed to be used as reference books. Libraries were designed to house reference books. Reference books were written so that people would not have to try to remember everything. Instead, when they need or want to know something, they can go look it up.

Schools teach children to act like walking reference books. Students who cannot do so automatically fail. It is not possible to motivate someone to develop a good memory when the person just naturally does not have one. It is a useless waste of time for students to try to become something they cannot be. Even if they could develop their memories it would not increase their learning abilities in any way. Memorizing and learning are two completely different functions that are mutually exclusive.

Modern education's approach to motivation always causes the less successful students to decrease their motivation to learn rather than increase it. Its methods leave students even more embittered and disinterested in school. For them, each day is agony, and every attempt to motivate them to do something that they cannot or will not do only makes matters worse. The fact that this system of motivation has failed completely has not deterred educators and school administrators from continuing their destructive and fruitless efforts.

For many children, this motivation method has been extremely damaging. A vast portion of children now attending school are actually losing their motivation to learn anything. They are becoming increasingly convinced that there is nothing out there for them that is worth learning. For many students it is as though the school officials and educators are beating them down. When the students get too beaten down, the school officials and educators call upon the parents to prop up the students. By the time students reach junior high and high school, they require more and more propping up from the parents. Most parents of high school students can attest to the fact that they need to work much harder to keep their sons and daughters in school than they did during the children's grammar school years. For some students it is as though their parents are holding them up while school officials and educators beat them down.

This description of how modern education attempts to motivate students is an understatement of the actual problem. The human consciousness is too limited to perceive or understand the full scope of destruction actually caused by these methods. Most readers will have difficulty comprehending what is being said here, because most readers are themselves products of modern education. They have already accepted the false conclusion that memory and intellect are the same thing. Most readers, because they are products of modern education, do not know what it would be like to actually be inspired to learn something. They have never had the experience of being motivated inside through inspiration. They only know about fear and punishment.

Very few readers have had any real experience of satisfaction in learning because schools offer so little that is worth learning. So if you happen to have been a student with a good memory, it was still not possible for you to derive real satisfaction from schoolwork, even if your grades were considered very good. In order to feel satisfied and motivated to greater learning, people must be involved in something that is worth accomplishing. Memorizing facts about history, for instance, has no value or meaning. It is therefore not worth doing and cannot yield inner satisfaction. Learning to build beautiful boats, on the other hand, might be well worth learning for some people. The results are tangible and useful.

Boatbuilding is potentially very satisfying because it has some inherent value.

Real motivation to learn anything always comes from inside of a person. It can never be conjured externally through fear and punishment, as modern education has attempted to do. Real motivation always grows out of an inner hunger to find out about something or to develop skills in a certain area. Inspiration to learn is often derived from seeing or experiencing someone manifesting a skill, or through observing and also absorbing the finished work of a master craftsperson.

If schools wanted to motivate students to learn and not just memorize, they would first need to provide students with subjects that are worth studying. These subjects would have to be relevant to life on this planet and would, in most cases, need to involve a tangible, useful result. Schools would offer courses in photography, welding, carpentry, boatbuilding, architectural design, plumbing, and auto mechanics. Schools would then need to employ master craftsmen in all of these areas who particularly enjoy watching other people work toward perfection.

The best way to then inspire students would be to surround them with beautiful, crafted works. Classrooms would contain magazine-quality photographs for the potential photographers, which could be observed and absorbed each day. Student carpenters would be surrounded with high quality, well-constructed cabinets, workbenches, desks, and other perfected projects. These finished products would demonstrate perfect joints and flawless finishes. The same would be true in every class where perfect, tangible results could be manifested.

Under these conditions, students could and would be motivated to learn, but only because they would hunger inside to produce beautiful, crafted, perfect results. Unfortunately, modern education knows nothing about beauty, craft, skill, or perfection. It reserves the Industrial Arts Department for students who have already failed and who are so destroyed by the system that they cannot be inspired.

Educational systems also fail to allow children to inspire one another. The schools keep children caught in a competitive structure which forces children to compete rather than help. Susie Jenkins loves spelling. Jimmy Rogers hates spelling, but has a natural desire to be able to spell. He learned to hate spelling because he is slower than his classmates and is chronically embarrassed by his low grades. Susie and Jimmy never get paired up so that Susie's natural ability for spelling can be mated with Jimmy's natural interest. Children are never given the opportunity to inspire and encourage each other to learn.

Standards of Measurement

We have already discussed the fact that modern education is based completely on memorization ability, and that grades only reflect a person's ability to memorize a given subject. Every year educational systems spend millions of dollars on measurement devices, as though these tests and exams actually measure learning. College entrance exams, medical and law school entrance exams, college midterms and finals, high school exams, weekly grammar school tests—all measure a person's ability to memorize and nothing else.

In order for education to measure actual learning, the system would have to shift from memorization to learning. This would mean that modern education would first have to provide students with something to learn, and then it could develop a system for measuring the amount of actual learning that had taken place. However, such a transition will not be possible for this system as it now exists, because it exists for the benefit of educators and school officials, not for the benefit of students.

If education existed for the benefit of students, there would be no tests or grades. These measurement systems only exist so that teachers can use the system to control children through fear and punishment. They can also pass off their own damages onto the children they claim to teach. If modern education today decided to do away with tests and grades (which it would never do) most current teachers and school officials would no longer have any interest in the system. They are generally attracted to education because it allows them to feel that they are the experts who can lord their expertise over the students. They have chosen their jobs for the power, authority, and feelings of personal importance that standing before a class allows them to have. They want authority and control over other people's lives, particularly children—who are rarely in a position to fight back. We have much more to say about teachers and school officials in this book. Here, We only wish to emphasize the fact that tests and grades do not measure learning, even though they continue to exist in schools. The underlying reason for their existence is that they allow teachers to dominate and control children through fear and punishment. Tests and grades allow teachers to pass their own inadequacies and failures onto their students so that they never have to look at themselves or their own lives.

Tests and grades are actually a way of teachers expressing their approval or disapproval of the students. Educators and school officials completely understand the vulnerabilities of the human ego structure. They use these weaknesses to control students by forcing the children to see themselves as either successes or failures within the school system. From either polarity the students can be controlled and manipulated. The successful students are controlled by their pattern of seeking the continuous approval of their teachers. These successful students, the ones with the good memories, have fallen for the idea that education offers them something, and that grades are a measure of a person's success and even self-worth. They use their memories to avoid punishment and humiliation, and to win the approval of educators and school officials.

At the other end of the scale, the unsuccessful students who cannot or will not memorize are similarly trapped as they seek the continuous disapproval of their teachers. The unsuccessful students usually succumb to feelings of personal failure and inadequacy when they discover that they do not have the memorization ability necessary to become successful students. They generally end up spending their inner resources trying to avoid these feelings of failure; and compensating for these feelings long into their adult lives.

As a result, most students leave high school with no inner ability to approve of themselves. They are completely dependent on the approval or disapproval of their parents, teachers, bosses, and friends. They have lost all natural ability to know who they are and what they want to do with their lives because they are so caught in other people's goals and expectations for them.

It is actually possible for people to measure learning. In fact, people who are doing things that produce tangible results in the physical world measure their own learning all the time. For instance, in order to become a plumber, one must apprentice with a master plumber. The apprentice works alongside the master plumber, observing the master's work and how it is accomplished. The apprentice observes and absorbs how pipes are laid and plumbing systems installed. If the apprentice is working with a true master, he or she observes and absorbs plumbing that is perfect.

These perfect results then become a target for which the apprentice must aim. He will measure his own work in reference to his target and decide for himself whether or not he is meeting his goals. The apprentice also measures his or her own success in terms of how the results have improved over time.

Boatbuilders do the same thing. They watch other skilled craftsmen and craftswomen and they see the boats produced by skilled boatbuilders. Over time, they measure the results of their own work by comparing their boats to those of the master craftsmen. They also measure their own learning as they begin, over time, to see success in certain areas. For example, a boatbuilder might discover that he or she is able to build perfect centerboard trunks or knees or transoms. Or, she might discover that she has mastered painting and varnishing a boat. Then, one day, after many years of learning, she may discover that she has, in fact, reached her target and produced a perfect boat.

Plumbers and boatbuilders do not need tests or grades to measure their work. They need experiences that will support them and allow them to learn. They do not need approval or disapproval if they are able to see plumbing perfectly installed, or extremely well-crafted boats being constructed. They are able to measure their own skills against what they see, and can then approve or not approve of what they are doing without any outside interference.

In reality, this is the only way that people can learn and measure their own learning. People never learn because they are tested and they never improve because they are graded. Modern education is a perfect no-learning system. By the time students graduate from high school, they have not only wasted twelve years memorizing, but the part of them that could have learned has been destroyed.

The current testing and measurement system has another dangerous side effect. When teachers test children on a subject, they usually record those grades. Those grades then become the basis for the students' report cards. However, teachers rarely give children the opportunity to go back and correct their mistakes so that their grades could be changed. Children are left with the clear impression that when they make mistakes they are stuck with those mistakes and are powerless to change them.

This remains embedded in every person's consciousness who

has been educated in this system. When people make mistakes in life, they do not see that they can fix those mistakes. They do not know how to end marriages that are not working, or how to change careers when they find out they dislike what they are doing. Some parents know they have made mistakes with their children but do not see that they can do and say things to correct those mistakes— in some cases even after their children have grown to adulthood.

People feel powerless to change their lives. They feel like they are only allowed one opportunity at a marriage, one chance at a career, and one time to parent their children. When these things fail or do not work out, people feel that they have flunked the test. It is too late. The grades have been recorded and they cannot go back and fix their mistakes, even though they often know exactly what to do to correct what they perceive as their errors.

If children were allowed to fail in a safe environment and to then correct their failures, people would live very different lives. When people get a second, third, or many chances to correct something, and can see the results of their corrections, they experience genuine satisfaction. In fact, it is only through failure and correction that satisfaction can actually be achieved. When children are forced into avoiding failure they are also forced into avoiding satisfaction, which is why so many educated people now lead such empty lives.

Classroom Decorum

When children go to school they are expected to sit in their seats and remain silent through most of the day. They are expected to sit up straight without slouching down in their chairs. They are not allowed to eat when they are hungry or laugh out loud when they think something is funny, except when a teacher tells a joke. Then, they are required to laugh. Children are not allowed to express their personal ideas or make suggestions for changing the classroom. They are not allowed to put their heads down, take a rest, or tell a teacher that they cannot learn any more that day because they are just too saturated.

In some schools children are not allowed to go to the bathroom when they need to go. They are not allowed to burp or to fart or to shout out loud or to cry.

As students grow older the negative discipline continues.

Women who are old enough to be having babies need a note from a teacher in order to walk through the halls between classes. Men who are old enough to die for their country in battle need notes from their mothers when they are late for school. Young adults who are old enough to drive cars, hold down jobs, or even start their own businesses, need a note from a teacher to use the bathroom.

Schools treat children like prisoners, only worse. Principals and teachers relate to high school students as though they were all severely retarded delinquents. No adult is treated in this way each day. There are no jobs in life that require people to behave this way, except perhaps for certain secretarial positions.

Children would have a much easier time in prison. In fact, prison life is much healthier than the average school situation. In prison, there are many more interesting things to do, and there is much more leisure time. No one expects prisoners to sit still all day pretending to listen to information about which they have no interest. No one fires constant questions at prisoners and expects them to feign interest and give answers, unless perhaps they are prisoners of the KGB.

Schools are worse than concentration camps. Children are required to remain seated all day and produce expressions of interest and passive acceptance of the teacher. Other expressions are not tolerated and are met with punishment. An improper expression in some school systems can land a student in the principal's office for a week at a time. Disagreeing with a teacher over a test grade can put a student in detention for a month.

Students have no say about who will teach them, whether their teachers are qualified, what subjects they will take, or what aspects of a subject they would like to learn. Teachers ridicule students who get bored in class. Yet, if you ask an English teacher why he or she is teaching English and not history, the teacher will most often say that he or she prefers English. However, students are not supposed to prefer anything. If they do not like English, they are supposed to keep quiet about that and pretend to like English. If a student tries to tell a teacher that he is not interested in a subject, the teacher will declare the student to be unmotivated. So although teachers choose a subject because they like it, and refuse to teach other subjects that they dislike, there is automatically something wrong with students who do not like something.

Schools claim to be teaching children to become better citizens.

But high school graduates generally do not know who is running their town or who is representing them in Congress. They are taught to vote for a democrat or a republican without ever knowing who the candidates are. Most cannot tell the difference between candidates who are telling the truth and those who are lying. What is worse is that most do not even care.

What people remember about school is what their teachers were like and how those teachers treated them. Most people who took French in high school cannot speak French today nor can they remember much about the language. However, most of them can tell you something about their French teachers. They can tell you whether their French teachers were tolerant or not, helpful or not, and whether or not those teachers liked their students.

In school, the medium is the message. If children are taught geography by someone who has never been around the world, they will learn about the world as a disconnected and fragmented place because that is what the world is to their teacher. If they are taught about civics from teachers who know nothing about government, they will learn to have the same unrelated, disconnected feelings toward government themselves.

What is it that students are learning in school? To become better citizens? Are they learning about democracy? If students were learning about democracy would they not have some say or vote about who should teach them, how much those teachers should be paid, and what subjects they want to pursue?

Are they learning about how to choose their leaders? School children learn that when someone is in authority you follow them blindly. You make the proper facial expressions and you make believe that you are interested in whatever that person says.

When young children sit before a teacher in a classroom, they often do not even perceive the fact that teachers are speaking to them. The fact that someone is talking to them or at them does not register inside most children as a communication. Since children between six and nine years of age are not ready to spend their time in classrooms, all of them (even the ones who perceive that they are being spoken to by the teacher) are faking their responses. These are the years when children should be out in the world experimenting and discovering what they want to do with their lives. What most children are learning in school is to fake it through life.

5

WHO TEACHES AND WHY

*NOTE: This is a book about reality. Reality is not positive.
Reality is extremely negative.*

Meet Emily

MEET EMILY SMITH, Teacher of the Year. Emily teaches the fifth grade class at Harrison Elementary School. In fact, she has been teaching fifth graders for the past eight years. This year Emily has been chosen by the Parent-Teacher Organization as the most out-standing educator in her school district. Soon she will be receiving a special plaque which will be awarded to her at a banquet in her honor. The plaque will read:

Teacher of the Year

*Awarded to Emily Smith in honor
of her dedication and commitment
to the education of our youth and
to the preparation of young minds
for productive roles in society.*

Each day Emily Smith teaches twenty-three fifth graders. Her day begins at 8:00 A.M. and ends at 2:00 P.M. During that six hour time period, Emily teaches grammar, spelling, arithmetic, science, geography, music, and reading. She is a confident and lively instructor, and is generally considered to be one of the best teachers the Harrison School has ever known.

Yet Emily, our 1988 Teacher of the Year, spends over half of her day sitting on a chair made from a type of wood she cannot identify. She has no idea how the lumber to make that chair was milled, nor could she tell you about the method used to hold the chair together. Emily does not know what kind of finish is covering the wood. She would not be able to explain what the construction of the chair has to do with mathematics, nor could she show you anything about the angles and bevels that give the chair its shape and form—even though she received all A's in her geometry courses.

Emily's desk is also constructed from wood, which she thinks is probably oak. Her desk has three large drawers with dovetail joints. She has no understanding about how this desk was put together, nor can she give you information on the way her desk blotter was constructed. She does not know how pencils are produced, or where the rubber for the pencil erasers originates.

Behind Emily's desk is a large blackboard with a ledge along the bottom to hold chalk and erasers. Emily cannot say where or how the blackboard was made, nor can she describe the method used to manufacture the chalk or erasers. She has no idea what materials were used to fasten the blackboard to the cement wall. She knows nothing about the process of constructing a wall, or about what actually holds up the building.

To the right of Emily's desk there are four big windows, each with sixteen panels of glass. Emily is unaware of how the windows were made, where the glass came from, or how to repair a window if a pane of glass should break. She cannot tell you the source of supply for the linoleum on the floor, or about how her two classroom doors were hung.

Emily's classroom is heated with oil. Emily knows that the oil is stored in large tanks in the school basement, but she is unfamiliar with the way oil is transferred from the tanks to the oil burner. And she cannot give you accurate information on how the oil burner functions to convert oil into heat for her classroom. She does not understand the system for regulating her classroom temperature, although she knows it has something to do with the thermostat located on the wall.

Her classroom is lit by fluorescent lights that are controlled by a panel of switches installed just to the left of the front entrance. Emily cannot tell you how the fluorescent lights were produced, nor does she know anything about wiring a room. She would be unable to find the circuit breakers for her classroom, or to render an opinion on whether her own house has a one hundred or two hundred amp service. She has never replaced a fuse, and does not recognize which wires in the fuse box are hot and which are ground—even though she just finished teaching the science unit on electricity.

The faculty lounge is located across the hall from Emily's classroom. In the lounge there is a coffeemaker and a small refrigerator. Emily has no idea how the refrigerator works to keep things cold. She can offer no information concerning the motor inside the refrigerator. In fact, her general knowledge about motors is very limited. Incidentally, she could not tell you anything about the coffeemaker either—except that when she pours cold water in the top and places ground coffee in the filter, hot coffee seems to come out the bottom.

The faculty bathrooms are located at the back of the lounge. Emily uses these facilities every day. She does not know the source of the toilet paper or paper towels, and she can explain very little about the plumbing in this room. She is not able to replace a washer in a faucet, or to fix a toilet if the tank will not refill. She thinks that plumbing is a job for the school custodian who is a very likable but "uneducated" man.

At the end of the school day, Emily will drive home in her white Subaru station wagon with the tan interior. She cannot describe how the brakes work. She only understands that when she depresses the brake pedal the car stops. She would not be able to change the oil in her car, nor can she change the spark plugs. In fact, she cannot even locate the spark plugs. She has no knowledge of how the gasoline is turned into energy which becomes motion. She is only aware that she must keep the car supplied with gas in order for it to run. Emily thinks that she might be able to change a flat tire, although she has never actually done it.

What is Emily Smith teaching her fifth graders about reality? How many times do you think her students will need to recite the Gettysburg Address? How many times do you think they will need to know how to repair a leaky faucet, or fix a broken toilet? How many times do you think her students will need to list ten bones in the human skeletal system from memory? How many times do you think her students will need to replace a blown fuse? How many times do you think Emily Smith's fifth graders will need to know the major exports of South America? And do you think that list might be different in the year 2007? How many times do you think her students will need to change a flat tire, balance a checkbook, or fill out an income tax form?

What exactly are Emily Smith's students being prepared to do with their lives?

Experts

Over ninety percent of the men and women involved in the educational system, as either educators or school administrators, are "experts." "Experts" are people who claim to know a great deal about life, but who, in the reality of the human world, actually know very little. "Experts" are people who want to look smart and appear important. They are people who are afraid to make mistakes or to be exposed as failures in any way.

"Experts" are actually very damaged, hurt people who have suffered some form of humiliation that was associated with making a mistake, or with failing at something important. They are often people who were damaged by the educational system themselves. The ones who became educators and school officials realized that as experts they would never again be the victims of the hurt and pain. Only their students are the victims. The students are the ones who live in fear, worry, and humiliation every day.

In order to avoid any further pain, educators and school administrators decided to enter the educational system where their roles would prevent them from suffering any further feelings of personal failure. When they came to these conclusions, however, they only shifted their role in the game. They would no longer be the victims, but could instead become the persecutors in a system that allows them to pretend they are the rescuers. They could be the ones who punished and humiliated children rather than being punished and humiliated themselves.

It should be noted here that not all "experts" (people who fear failure) become educators. Some go to graduate school so that they can acquire letters after their names. The letters protect them from confronting their personal failures. People become M.D.'s, Ph.D.'s, D.D.S.'s, M.Ed.'s, M.S.W.'s, and M.B.A.'s. The doctoral programs attract those people who have been the most ruined by education. These are the people who have their self-worth tied up with the doctoral degrees that hang on their walls, and who want to use these degrees to gain power over other people so they will never have to look at themselves. Ironically, these are the people with the least expertise. How many schizophrenics has your favorite psychiatrist or psychologist cured this year? What can your favorite doctor of divinity tell you about the requirements for the seven planetary initiations? The real experts are the plumbers, welders, and electricians who have to prove their expertise on the job each day. If society wanted to award doctoral degrees, these are the men and women who should receive the Ph.D.'s. Instead, these are the people to whom educators assign no value or worth—except, of course, when their pipes burst or their electricity fails.

The men and women who enter the field of education do so primarily to pass along their damages and feelings of personal failure to the children they claim to want to teach. Those few men and women who do enter the field of education with a sincere interest in young children are rarely able to survive within the system. They are the ones who usually leave because they feel blocked from making the changes that would be necessary for children to learn and grow. They quickly discover that the educational system forbids such changes. "Experts" in any field do not want to be threatened. They do not want changes that could expose them to feelings of personal failure, or cause them to look at the fact that they might have made a mistake. They are people who have constructed their lives around avoiding failure. Yet, the educators and school officials want to be seen as people who change, so they change the textbooks every few years, or they change the audio-visual aids, or the location of the desks in the classroom. However, they never institute change that would allow students to thrive and to grow.

Five hundred years ago the Flat Earth Society considered itself humanity's experts. The Flat Earthers were convinced beyond any doubt that the world was flat and linear, and that the universe was constructed in single straight lines. The Flat Earthers did not want to hear any evidence to the contrary.

The Flat Earthers were to the physical world what educators are to the mental world, and religious leaders are to the spiritual world. Educators are the "flat earthers" of the human mind. They want everything to exist in flat, linear form. They want to relate to the world as if they could control it and fix it in one place. They do not want to allow any evidence that runs contrary to their fixed ideas about education and the human mind, in the same way that religious leaders do not want their "flat earth" religious fantasies interrupted.

"Experts" are people who do not wish to look at themselves or at what they are doing. They want other people to perceive them as knowledgeable and important. They support their self-importance by watching other people fail. Classrooms are perfect places for experts who want to watch children fail so that they can feel important.

It has been mentioned earlier in this book that people learn through failure. Again, the type of failure We were referring to is the kind people experience when they discover that the way they are attempting to fit a boat part, for instance, just will not work. They must then invent a way that will work. This is failure without any form of interference or punishment, that actually produces learning and growth.

Educators have failed their students. When Madeline lies on her bed crying because she has discovered that her husband is more interested in football than in her, what has education taught her that will help her? When Bill gets fired from his job after thirty years of dedicated work, what has education taught him that will help him? When Joe and Susan's first baby is stillborn, what has education taught them that will help?

Everyone knows that education has failed them, which is why teachers are so poorly paid. People hold educators in contempt. Surely, in theory, the educator's role in society is as important as the doctor's role or the lawyer's role? Why then do people pay their doctors and lawyers so much more money than they pay to their educators? People feel that doctors help them. They even feel that lawyers help them, even though they know that most lawyers are not very honest people because they are part of the underbelly of society. People feel that educators have failed them which, of course, they have. People also know that education has not been good for them, although they are not always able to pinpoint how or why. Humanity has disdain for educators and school officials. They only need to look at the educators' paychecks and compare those with their favorite physicians' and attorneys' salaries to know that what We say here is true. People do not want to pay teachers to destroy their children, even though people would not always be able to know this consciously.

Black Hats and White Hats

In the cowboy movies of the 1950s, the good guys wore the white hats and the bad guys wore the black hats. The good guys saved the women and children while the bad guys pillaged and robbed the town. Everyone clearly knew which cowboys were the good guys and which were the bad.

However, in times of darkness the good guys and the bad guys are not usually so clearly defined. There are always obvious bad guys, like Hitler and Stalin, who do such barbaric and destructive things to their own societies that it is clear they mean harm. Often in the course of doing harm, men like Stalin and Hitler come up with a few positive results which go unnoticed because their destructive acts are so tragic.

When the Jews stood before the Nazis, they knew what color hats the Nazis were wearing. The Jews knew that they were standing before people who intended to kill them, and that they could do nothing except be killed. When a person stands before his killer and knows he will be annihilated, that person dies with dignity. The intention to harm and destroy is clear and the results are even clearer.

When young children go off to school, they are not so fortunate. They are placed in a system that purportedly will teach them all they need to know about life. They are told that school is a beneficial place, and that teachers are people who want to help them learn and grow. Children expect school to be a good experience because they are told these things by the people they love and trust the most in the whole world—their parents.

In reality, school is not a positive place, and teachers are usually not people who want to help children learn and grow. If teachers wanted to help children learn, they would not test them or grade them or embarrass them in any way. If teachers wanted to help children, they would cater to all the learning needs of all their students, not just the three to five percent who have good memories.

If teachers really wanted to help children they would look at the fact that natural reality clearly indicates people learn at different rates of speed. To test a class of students on a given subject is to assume that everyone learns everything at exactly the same rate, and in exactly the same way. Of course teachers know this is not true. They know that when they test their students, only a very few will have learned everything that was presented. The remainder of the class will be punished with less than perfect grades, or even failing grades, so that the teachers can pass their damages on to the children.

Natural reality also indicates that people have different interests at different times. If people did not have different interests, then everyone would be doing the same thing. Fortunately, some people are attracted to medicine while others prefer farming, plumbing, or photography. Teachers know that children have varied interests, and that most children are not interested in what is being offered at school. They know because they have to embarrass some children to make them study. Sometimes they even call in the parents to help force the children into what they do not naturally want to do.

These are insidious conditions because the bad guys are hard to identify. When a Nazi soldier killed a Jew, the Jew died with dignity because he knew the enemy for what he was. The murder was clearly a barbaric act. However, when a teacher fails a student in the name of good education, the student loses all dignity because no one admits that the enemy is attacking him. The attack is insidious because it not only causes the child to feel destroyed, but he also cannot even clearly identify his destroyer. His parents, whom he thought were his friends, have already sided with the enemy, and he is left without recourse.

When teachers fail and punish children in school, they commit a violent act. It is not physically violent in the way that the Nazis were violent, but it is a mental act of war on another's consciousness. When teachers fail students and punish them, they are deciding that only the fittest shall survive. The fittest in this case are not even the great intellects or inventors, but instead the people with good memories.

The Soviet Union is a nation which suppresses its adults. It is a country where adults are not yet free to do what they want whenever they want to do it. Most Americans condemn the Soviet system for this suppression. Yet, in America the children are also suppressed. They are suppressed in ways that are far more serious than those inflicted upon adults in the Soviet Union. In America, children are placed in the hands of people who want to punish them and embarrass them. They are destroyed because they cannot learn at the same rate as others, or because they do not have any interest in the subjects being taught.

The Societal Veil

Educators, like religious leaders, are protected by veils assigned by society. These societal veils allow educators and religious leaders to hide behind the protective covering of their roles in society, without being held accountable for their actual words and behaviors. For instance, ministers, priests, and rabbis are some of the most disturbed people in society. They are people who lived very isolated, alienated lives as children and have grown up in very disturbed family systems. If some of them were not protected by these societal veils, their psychological disturbances would be so severe that they would require psychiatric treatment.

Most religious leaders have serious problems with their personal relationships. Many suffer from depression, alcoholism, and other problems that stem from their inability to relate to other people. In a time of darkness, religious leaders were supposed to help keep the idea of God alive. Instead, most ministers and priests have learned to pretend that they are the gods. They stand before their congregations and claim that they can do things to help people which they are simply incapable of doing.

Imagine any of today's televangelists standing before people and saying,

> *I'm here to tell you about Jesus because I think what he did is important to remember. Jesus lived a life of service and self-sacrifice. While he was alive, he did everything he could to help other people. I think he was trying to tell us to do the same thing. So far, I have not been able to do what Jesus did. See my diamond ring, my gold watch, my six-hundred-dollar suit? Jesus did not waste his life on these things, but so far I have not been able to do any better than this.*
>
> *I'm telling you about Jesus because I think it is important*

to look at how he lived. Some of you might be able to do
better than I have done.

In saying this, the televangelists would be keeping the idea of
God alive. They would not be pretending to perform miracles, nor
would they be trying to convince people that they were at all like
Jesus.

However, societal veils allow ministers and priests to pretend
they are humble men and women who are like Jesus. Everyone
knows that religious leaders are disturbed and even corrupt. It is
only recently that anyone has attempted to expose the disturbance
and corruption. For more information about religions and religious
leaders, see Volume II of this series, *Modern Religion and the*
Destruction of Spiritual Capacity.

Educators are also hidden from society. When very disturbed
teachers humiliate and punish children, they are rarely exposed.
School administrators and parents almost always side with the
teacher, as if something was wrong with the children rather than
the teacher. Most parents automatically blame their children for
not being able to adjust to school, rather than questioning the
methods or motives of any school personnel.

When children are abused and destroyed by teachers, parents
pretend that it is all part of getting a good education. They do not
confront the insanity behind the educational system. This system
is policed by the teachers and school administrators so that no one
ever confronts the reality of the destruction that is taking place.

We would suggest that people make a list of all the qualities
they would want to find in a teacher. These are the qualities that
people project onto the societal veil which protects the teachers
from any confrontation with reality. These qualities might include
compassion, understanding, nurturance, resourcefulness, inventiveness, imagination, intelligence, competency, and stability.
Since this is the human world where almost everything is seen
backward, these qualities cannot actually be found in over ninety
percent of all educators.

Now make a list of the qualities that you would not want to
find in a teacher. These might include being negative, destructive,
hurtful, abusive, withholding, self-centered, incompetent, dishonest, or of limited intelligence. Since this is the human world, you
have just described most of today's educators.

Parents who believe that harsh treatment of children makes for a good education are seriously mistaken. With very few exceptions, anyone who would test or grade a child wants to hurt children. Whenever a teacher tests or grades a child, it is done out of damage and unresolved personal pain, with very few exceptions. Parents who believe that child abuse builds character when it is done in school are seriously mistaken. They cannot begin to imagine the harm that is inflicted in the name of a good education.

Teacher Competence and Evaluation

It is impossible for a competent teacher to emerge from an organized teacher training program. Even the few who enter these programs with any remaining natural gifts that might be useful in the teaching profession are quickly filled with meaningless ideas about lesson plans, study guides, reading grade levels, curriculum planning, and performance testing. Teachers are products of their own incompetent, disturbed system—a system which teaches no skills and nothing about the real world.

As has been discussed, education attracts damaged people who fear failure and do not want to look foolish. Because education is an incompetent, disturbed system, it not only attracts damaged people, but incompetent, disturbed damaged people. It is a system that breeds and fosters incompetence in children by placing them in the hands of inept, incompetent adults.

Teachers are not required to prove any level of skill or accomplishment in their field. They are policed and evaluated by other incompetent people who use meaningless standards to evaluate performance. Teacher evaluation systems are as meaningless as student report cards. Student report cards reflect only the student's ability to memorize. Nothing else is measured in the classroom but memory. Teacher evaluations measure meaninglessness. They reflect a teacher's ability to incorporate meaningless ideas such as lesson plans, curriculum, and grade level evaluations, and to expand these meaningless concepts into something that can be inflicted upon children.

As a result, education attracts meaningless, boring, incompetent people. Anyone who has attended a school assembly where teachers and school administrators controlled the podium can tell you this is true. In the process of training to become teachers, any spark of imagination, or good intentions to inspire children, is completely lost. There are no standards of skill or requirements for competence included in any teacher preparation program.

If you had an electrical problem in your home that required the attention of an electrician, you would probably seek a qualified master electrician. You would want a person who had demonstrated his or her ability in physical reality, and had received the certification and approval of someone with a high degree of skill in the field of electricity. Most likely you would not consider hiring someone who told you that he could do the job because he had been studying about electricity from science books over the past four years. You would not want someone who—though he had never actually wired a house—had memorized all the definitions that a person in his field would want to know.

Teachers are given control of children's lives based on the assumption that they are qualified to work with children after merely reading books about teaching and memorizing all the educational jargon necessary to function in the school system. In the course of their training, most teachers only work directly with children for a few months, and only in settings where they are monitored by incompetent, unskilled teachers.

People are much more demanding of their plumbers and electricians than they are of their teachers. People look closely at the work of the electricians and the plumbers. They can verify the electrician's work by turning on a lamp to see if it is working or not. They can verify the plumber's work by flushing the toilet to see if it is working or not. If the lamp does not light or the toilet does not flush, you can be certain that people will complain and demand competent service.

Yet, no one looks at the fact that most high school graduates have not learned how to handle a car safely, fill out a tax return, administer emergency first aid, take care of a new baby, relate to a marriage partner, or manage grocery shopping for a family. No one questions the fact that more and more children and teenagers are using drugs than ever before, in spite of Nancy Reagan's "Say No" campaign. No one questions the fact that teen-age suicide rates are steadily rising, and that many of those who do take their own lives had great difficulty in school. No one questions the fact that teenagers and younger children are dressing in disturbed-looking clothes and wearing bizarre hair styles. No one asks that teachers produce healthy and competent high school graduates.

Education produces poor results year after year. If the electrician or the plumber produced poor results, he or she would quickly go out of business. Yet, the educational system has only become more popular as it has become more destructive. Parents are sending their children off to school at much earlier ages, and some states are considering year round schools. This, incidentally, would be the final nail on the coffin for most children who are now able to make some recovery from the school year during their summer vacations.

Teachers demand to be obeyed. They demand that children submit to their authority and show them respect, whether they have earned it or not. Most teachers do not deserve to be obeyed. Most have not demonstrated any real qualities of leadership, integrity, or interest in the well-being of children. What they have displayed is authority, which is all that is necessary when your primary goal is to frighten children into submission.

The Glass Slipper Game

All teachers play the "glass slipper" game whether they want to play or not. The game is so institutionalized that even the best teachers end up choosing their favorite Cinderellas or Cinderfellas. The way this game works is that the educational system has certain criteria which children must meet in order to succeed in the classroom. These criteria, especially a good memory, have already been discussed. All of the students with good memories automatically become potential Cinderellas or Cinderfellas.

Additionally, each individual teacher has criteria which to him or her constitute the ideal student. Some teachers like boys better than girls. Some teachers prefer quiet children to talkative children. Some teachers like very passive children more than they like ambitious or aggressive children. Some teachers are partial to children who do a lot of extra work while others consider those children "brown-nosers." Some teachers like math more than any other subject, so they like students who are good in math. Other teachers prefer history and tend to favor students who are also interested in history.

Each year the child who meets the established criteria, who can most easily fit into the individual teacher's idea of the good student, wins the glass slipper and becomes the favored student for that year. Some people call these favored students "teachers' pets."

This term is quite accurate since most teachers award the glass slipper to the students who are most willing to act like obedient puppies seeking only to please their masters.

The winner of the glass slipper one year may not win the next year. The fact that a student has a good memory is not enough to insure this award. Teachers have many individual, varied criteria for what they would call an ideal student. A student who is very appealing to one teacher may have no appeal to another. This is why the "best" student in the class can vary so much from year to year.

Teachers also play the rubber boot game. This game is also institutionalized and is played by every teacher whether they intend to play it or not. Every school has a set of criteria for establishing the worst students in the school. These are the children who either cannot or will not memorize the data presented to them, and who are perceived by the school system as the problem children.

Each individual teacher also has a list of criteria for what he or she finds distasteful. Some teachers like thin children better than fat children. Some like short children better than tall children. Some prefer children who are more materially fortunate and dislike children who are poor. Some teachers perceive themselves as very good reading teachers and feel contempt for children who do not readily learn to read. The list is as long as there are human preferences.

Each year the students who have already been designated as problem children or "slow learners" compete for the rubber boot award. The child who wins the rubber boot is the one who most clearly represents the qualities which that individual teacher dislikes in a child and in a student. This is the child who can expect to be humiliated and punished more than any other child in the class throughout the year.

The rubber boot award, like the glass slipper, does not necessarily go to the same child every year. The receiver of the rubber boot award changes from year to year, depending on each individual teacher's personal preferences. Always the winner is the one for whom the teacher has the most contempt. In order to stay in the teacher's good graces, most students in the class also express contempt and disdain for the winner of the rubber boot award, even children who might be his or her best friends outside of the classroom. The winner of the rubber boot award usually cannot wait for the year to be over so that the award will once again be up for grabs. The glass slipper recipient, on the other hand, often has a very difficult time when someone else receives the award the following year. The glass slipper recipients have a painfully difficult time adjusting to the loss of the role as classroom Cinderella or Cinderfella.

Children at both ends of the spectrum are damaged by these roles. No award winner escapes some form of mental-emotional pain. Every teacher knows that the game is being played. Every teacher knows that the children involved are being injured, but no one has the resources to stop the game because it is as institutionalized as the educational system itself.

Natural Instinct and Skill

If you are an educator or a school official, or have been one in the past, you have probably come to the conclusion that this information does not describe you. You have most likely concluded that you are one of those very few exceptional teachers who does or has done a competent job at meeting the needs of the children in the classroom. If you have reached this conclusion, then you are one of the ninety percent of educators and school officials who are dedicated to destroying children. You are one of the "experts" whose system is so airtight that you cannot allow yourself to see how incompetent and unskilled you really are. You are one of the ninety percent who is so completely convinced that what you are doing to children is acceptable that you have no room to see another point of view. You are one of the dangerous ones who year after year does the same destructive things to children in the name of a good education.

If you are an educator or school official who has read to this point in the book, and you now feel a deep hurt in your heart for what you have been doing with children, you are probably one of the rare exceptions mentioned in this chapter. If you have always harbored a bad feeling about what happens to children in schools, you probably belong in the classroom. If this information makes you feel sick to your stomach, and reminds you of the feeling you have always had that you are not doing enough for your students, then you probably belong in a classroom.

If you are one of the exceptions to what has been said here, you probably will not be able to teach in the current system for very long. Anyone who shows signs of being a competent teacher, or tries teaching children something about reality, is usually given all the disturbed and needy students. These students are the ones who quickly drain competent teachers of their resources so that they have nothing left to teach with, and therefore burn out within a few short years. This happens regularly in Industrial Arts Departments. All the problematic children and teenagers end up here where the only courses connected to reality are being taught. By the time they arrive in industrial arts, these students have been so destroyed by the system that they are too devastated and needy to be able to benefit from the courses. Instead, they are used by the schools to burn out the industrial arts teachers.

In order for anyone to be competent and skilled in the classroom, the person must possess certain natural, instinctive gifts that would allow him or her to work successfully with children. The natural, instinctive part of each human being is the part that senses reality without using the mind. It is the part of a person which senses, for instance, when someone is telling the truth and when someone is lying. This instinctive part of each person is the only part that can determine such things. How education destroys that instinctive part of people by the time they have reached the second grade will be discussed further along in this book.

Here, We want only to say that this instinctive part of people is the only part that could develop into a competent teacher. In a classroom of twenty-five children, no two children have the same needs or interests. And no two children have the same learning requirements. Everyone is different. Certain children might really need to be yelled at from time to time in order to wake up some part of themselves that is capable of learning. Those who do need to be yelled at need it only at certain times, and only from that part of the teacher that loves them and wants the best for them. Yelling at children from any other place, or for any other reason, is always destructive.

Other children would feel destroyed if someone yelled at them, even someone who loved them and wanted the best for them. In the current system everything is backward. The natural instinctive part of teachers has generally been destroyed. Teachers, like students, have reached the conclusion that all their own natural abilities to learn are of no value. They have instead decided that the human mind is valuable. Unfortunately, the mind has no instinctive ability. It reads reality backward. Consequently, the children who need to be yelled at in order to learn, cannot get yelled at to save their lives. The children who are devastated by someone yelling at them get yelled at every day. And it comes from the part of the teacher that wants to harm the child because the teacher himself has been hurt.

This is only one small example. Children's needs are as varied and as individual as the number of children in the classroom. Teachers imagine that it would be too overwhelming and chaotic to try to meet these needs. However, the reality is that not meeting children's needs produces much more chaos and overwhelms children much faster than teachers can possibly imagine.

When people's natural instincts are destroyed they approach the world from the human mind, which gives them false data about the world. College professors approach the world completely from the educated human mind. Consequently, they are some of the most disturbed people in society. They are often so specialized in their expertise that they are incapable of carrying on a normal dinner table conversation. They are so detached from the real world that they rarely maintain successful marriage or family relationships.

When people approach life from the mind, they most often end up in the wrong jobs. People who should be farming cannot receive any encouragement or support to become farmers. People who should be painting never get near an easel or paint brush. People who belong in the classroom teaching cannot get into the school system. People who have the natural interests and abilities to relate to children and to help them learn cannot locate those natural abilities once they have been educated. Therefore, the people who do end up in classrooms are not only damaged and incompetent, but usually have no natural connections or relationships with children. Most educators do not even like being around children, and should not be in a classroom even if their damages were healed. However, education in the human world means that everything is turned backward. So the people most naturally qualified to teach children cannot be found in the classroom.

Some professions are able to provide people with decent training. Electricians, auto mechanics, physicians, and bartenders, for example, are people who can get reasonably good training. Electronics technicians, boatbuilders and machinists can also get reasonably good training. Lawyers, educators, politicians, and business people, however, are not as fortunate. These are areas of work that require special talents. The professional training programs that have been organized for people aspiring to these careers are substandard at best. For educators, these training programs are dangerously inferior. The problem is that people have not been able to determine what natural talents and skills should be found in a competent teacher or lawyer. Educational institutions respond to their own ignorance by firing information at these people. These institutions think that if you open the choke on the shotgun and fire enough pellets at educators and lawyers in training, something is bound to hit the person in a way that will cause the desired effect. As a result, teachers come out of their own training programs full of holes. They then try the same shotgun approach to education on vulnerable children in the confinement of their classrooms.

A Test for Teachers

You have just survived a nuclear holocaust. You are the only teacher left on the planet, and your job is to rebuild the school.

1. *Could you make a pencil?* _____

2. *Could you construct a blackboard?* _____

3. *Could you make an eraser?* _____

4. *Could you find a piece of chalk?* _____

5. *Could you build a desk?* _____

6. *Could you put together a chair?* _____

7. *Could you make paper?* _____

8. *Could you print and bind a book?* _____

9. *Could you build a school?* _____

10. *Could you install the bathrooms?* _____

11. *Could you wire the classrooms?* _____

12. *Could you make and install a heating system?* _____

13. *Could you produce a window?* _____

14. *Could you hang a door?* _____

15. *Could you lay a floor?* _____

16. *Could you build stairs?* _____

17. *Could you make a coat rack?* _____

18. *Could you make a clock?* _____

19. *Could you construct worktables for the students?* ___

20. *Could you level and tar the schoolyard?* _____

21. *Could you build a fence?* _____

22. *Could you produce a flag?* _____

23. *Could you turn a flagpole on a lathe?* _____

24. *Could you make a pen?* _____

6

MIND REPLACES INSTINCT

NOTE: This is a book about reality. Reality is not positive. Reality is extremely negative.

THROUGHOUT THIS BOOK We have spoken about the damaging effects of modern education on the lives of children and educated adults. We are not able to fully communicate the seriousness of this damage in a way that people could understand. People have been living under the influence of religious and educational fantasies for so long that they are simply unequipped to comprehend the full destruction that has taken place. In a way, We can reveal only the most obvious forms of destruction, because even this is a difficult pill to swallow.

If We were to isolate the single most devastating effect of education on the human consciousness, it would be the breakdown of all natural instinctive abilities and the substitution of the overused, overloaded human mind. The fact that teachers themselves have lost all their own natural instincts has already been discussed. Most educators are in the wrong jobs, doing the wrong things. The few who do belong in the classrooms are unable to respond to children's needs because they have lost all instinctive ability to do so. Most educators are too damaged even to know what this means, and certainly would not be able to change it.

Children in the very early years of school quickly discover that their natural abilities to learn will not be useful in the classroom setting. They discover that who they are as individuals and how they learn are not relevant in the system that claims to want to educate them. They quickly learn through embarrassment and punishment that their personal interests are of no concern to their teachers. Their individual ideas, inventions, goals, feelings, and needs have no place in the classroom.

Schools own all the ideas. Teachers' feelings, goals, and interests are the only ones that count. The teacher's methods of teaching are the only thing of value, not the student's methods of learning. The schools not only own all the ideas, they even own the books. Students use the books, but they rarely ever get to take them home at the end of the school year. Even if they do, the books have no meaning so they are not cherished or regarded in any positive way. College students buy their books but sell them without reluctance at the end of each semester because the books have no value. The ideas contained in them do not belong to the students.

By the time they reach the second grade it is very clear to most students that they must abandon all their own natural instinctive abilities to learn in order to survive in the classroom setting. Their feelings, goals, and needs have no value, and they must conform to the ruling interests of their teachers. Children conclude that to survive in school they must rely completely on the human mind. They must be willing to memorize all the information they can, whether they have any interest or connection with it or not.

When natural interests are suppressed in children, these interests turn into unnatural needs for excitement and stimulation. The more the natural interests are suppressed, the more a person will try unsuccessfully to rekindle them through unnatural excitement. People who faithfully watch television game shows, soap operas, and nighttime dramas like "Dallas" are the ones with the broken spirits. They hunger for real learning, but they feel starved for excitement. The same thing is true about people who follow television ministries where ministers sing, yell, preach, pace, and arouse emotion—which is very exciting, but completely useless.

Once children conclude that their natural interests are useless, they begin to rely on their minds for data that can only be received through their hearts. As We have said, the only way for a person to judge the character or sincerity of another person is through intuition or natural instinct. Educated people have very little judgment ability left. It is much easier to fool an educated person than it is to fool someone who has not been contaminated by education. Uneducated children from the Ozarks are much more able to accurately read the character, or lack of it, in another person than the educated stockbrokers of Wall Street.

These disturbances in judgment, resulting from education's destruction of simple human instinct, are most evident in America's political choices. Most Americans have no ability to determine which of the men and women running for political office are people of good will, and which are not. When children's instincts are destroyed and they are forced to submit to the authority of teachers—many of whom lack character and a proper value system—they can no longer determine sincere leaders from power-hungry fakes and frauds. All that is necessary for a person to become President of the United States is that the person have enough charisma to face the American people and enough ambition to want the job. Most people now in government in the Western world achieved their positions because they were hungry for power, not because they wanted to serve their people. Margaret Thatcher is one of the few exceptions to this statement and she is not at all popular among her people. The world leaders who sought their positions to achieve personal power are by far much more popular.

A perfect example of this phenomenon can be found in America's response to Oliver North. During the entire Iran-Contra hearings, he feigned sincerity with little boy faces and puppy dog eyes. He clearly admitted deceiving and lying to people in his work. Americans responded to him as though he were sincere and as though he were a man of character. American people are so educated that they can no longer determine the difference between character and charisma. As a result, men like Oliver North, and people from the Watergate scandal, become the nation's heroes. They write books that glamorize their deceptive and corrupt behaviors. People buy and read this trash as though it deserved to be immortalized and incorporated into people's lives. Dean, Erlichman, Liddy, and others are popular speakers at colleges and other lecture circuits. Since these men committed their crimes, they have become popular American heroes in the same way that Oliver North is now being glamorized.

While America extols the heroes of Watergate and the Iran hearings, people like Mitch Snyder cannot raise enough interest or money to obliterate homelessness in a single city. Some people reading this book do not even know who Mitch Snyder is, but every reader in the Western world can probably tell you something about Oliver North.

People will spend money on bestsellers written by corrupt political leaders, by football players who write stories about how they have destroyed another man's career on the ball field, or by movie stars who write about disturbed and meaningless marriages. However, they will not send a dime to help midwestern farmers get back on their feet. They will do nothing to help Mother Teresa in India, nor will they do anything to help feed the starving children of Ethiopia. They will not because education has destroyed their instincts to help and to do the right thing simply because it is the right thing.

If the United States was doing its job and fulfilling its purpose as a nation, it would be teaching the world about truthfulness. Because America is destined to fulfill this purpose, American liars in public office tend to get exposed more than liars from other nations' governments. However, instead of consciously attending to the truth, America today glorifies its liars like Nixon and North, and glamorizes the Fawn Hall's and Donna Rice's who expose them.

In addition to destroying human instincts, modern education causes serious depression in most children. Before attending school, children live in an active world with pace and momentum, unless they are being neglected in some serious way. During these early years, children are naturally stimulated by their parents and the world around them. This stimulation is partially responsible for the active pace and momentum of life to which children become naturally accustomed.

Then children go to school where they are forced to sit still and be quiet. The vital and life-giving pace and momentum come to a screeching halt. The vast majority of children cannot tolerate this severe and very negative change in their lives. The only way they can adjust to classroom life is to become depressed. Most children stay depressed long into their adult lives. Some remain permanently depressed as a result of this abrupt severing from the active world.

Any parent who can remember how his or her child looked before starting school can tell you that this description is true. All parents see this dejection and unhappiness in their children. Generally, people simply consider this reaction to be a normal response to "growing up" and going to school.

Depression may be normal but it is not natural. And if people consider the world that most young preschool children have experienced, depression can be seen as a particularly unnatural response.

If people want to incarcerate their children for twelve years, it would be much more humane to begin the incarceration immediately following birth. It would be much easier on children to never experience an active, stimulating world with pace and momentum than to be ripped away from that active, alive world and incarcerated in passive, dead classrooms. If parents incarcerated their children right after birth the children would still have problems, but none as painful as they now know. It would be much more natural for children never to experience the early contact with parents or with life that stimulates and vitalizes, if they are destined only to have it all stripped away from them in the name of education.

Educators claim that schools do stimulate children, and there is truth in this claim. However, schools stimulate none of the natural, instinctive learning abilities in children—which is why classroom life has no pace or momentum. Schools only stimulate children's linear minds, and even then it is negative stimulation.

In short, this system causes children to substitute what they can remember for what they already know. What they intuitively and instinctively know has no value in school. All emphasis is placed only on what they can remember. Once students substitute what they remember for what they know—usually by the third grade—they can no longer relate to reality.

Lost Vision

As children begin to live their lives through their minds, their lives become very blurry. It is as though they are looking out at the world through a camera lens that is not in focus. No matter how hard they try, they cannot get the world into focus because the camera itself is broken. Children whose instincts and natural interests are destroyed do not know what they want or how they feel. They no longer know what their parents want from them, or even what their teachers expect them to do beyond memorizing their textbooks.

Between the first and fifth grades, children are driven further and further from reality. They are locked up in classrooms, far away from anything going on outside in the real world. They attend schools that are run like prisons. No one enters a school building without permission, even though schools are supposed to be public buildings, just like town halls. No one can get in because no one is allowed to tamper with the process of driving children away from themselves and from all physical reality.

Before nine or ten years of age, children can discover who they are only by anchoring themselves into the physical world. It is the only way for children to discover who they are and what they need out of the physical world. It is also the only way they can discover how they personally can contribute to that world.

Modern education is built on the assumption that children between ages five and eighteen have no interest in life. It assumes that children of these ages have no interest in the world and no desire to make a contribution to that world. Based on these assumptions, education flips children into the mental world. Many kindergarten and first grade children are shocked by this experience. They had started to anchor themselves naturally into the physical world, but as soon as they began school their anchors were ripped up as though they had been tossed into a violent storm at sea. People need only look at the faces of five, six, and some seven-year-olds to see the shock and violence that has been inflicted on them.

By the time children reach the fifth and sixth grades, they are numb and vulnerable. Their visions of life have become even more blurry, and some have faded completely into unconsciousness. The educational system sees the vulnerability in these children. It responds to this vulnerability by placing some of the most damaged and destructive teachers in these grades. These teachers are like sharks who see a wounded prey and come in for the final kill. By the end of the sixth grade, the destruction is complete. Very few students have any consciousness left by the time they enter the seventh grade.

Once this destruction of natural instincts and interests occurs it cannot be repaired except in rare cases under extremely protected circumstances. For the general population of Western society, it would be accurate to say that people have been destroyed by education in such a way that they simply cannot be repaired, no matter what they do with their lives.

When unconscious, numb children grow up and graduate from high school they become unconscious, numb adults. They have no connection to what they want to do with their lives. They only have inaccurate, disturbed mental ideas about making money and becoming successful, which are the lowest possible forms of human accomplishment. These aspirations cause even the most basic human survival systems to break down in society.

For example, in the animal kingdom there are obvious innate survival systems. These systems are literally built into the animal's physical construction. Birds that need to travel great distances to obtain ample food supplies are equipped to fly such distances. Fish that must survive on certain other ocean animals are equipped to locate, capture, and digest those creatures.

The human kingdom was also constructed for survival. The first system that insures human survival is the grouping of people together into families to share the load. This system has been disturbed because people are choosing the wrong mates and attracting the wrong children. The family system was meant to function as a cooperative unit in which people shared the burdens of survival. Most families are too busy coping with their own disturbances to offer each other any relief from the difficulties of having to survive.

The second system for survival in the human kingdom is built into each individual consciousness. Each consciousness is equipped to naturally attract resources of all kinds in a specific and certain way. Each consciousness is equipped with certain natural abilities combined with astrological influences that will naturally attract the resources it needs in order to survive. This is true even for the welfare mother with four children. Although people would not necessarily become wealthy, this system would cause the proper distribution of resources among the people of the world if it was functioning correctly.

Education has interfered in the functioning of this system so that people cannot uncover this aspect of themselves. They do not know this aspect of the consciousness even exists. People are so numbed and unconscious by the time they leave high school that they live like mental robots. They move through life by following fads. Fads are all human ideas that lead nowhere, which is why they all die out. People live so completely on their ideas that they do not know how to use their time or gather resources.

The third system for survival of the human race is the warning alarm system. This system is designed to send out signals to the world that the other two systems have failed. Now the alarms are sounding. Poverty is increasing. Homelessness is on the rise. Adolescent suicide is growing. Mental illness is rampant. Drug problems increase each year and affect younger and younger children. AIDS is epidemic in the world. Unfortunately, no one can hear the alarms because education put everyone to sleep long ago.

The Mind

Educators are the ones who speak so often about the value of the human mind. They are like the religious leaders who rant and rave about salvation through Jesus Christ. In the human world where almost everything is reversed, the educators are actually destroying the human mental vehicles, while the priests and ministers work hard at destroying humanity's spiritual capacity.

Educators are famous for saying that "a mind is a terrible thing to waste." In reality, it is far more terrible to misuse and overload the human mind than it would be to waste it. In fact, one might say that the greatest waste of the human mind is to overload it and misuse it.

The linear mind was actually designed to function like a memory storage disk in a computer. People learn about life through direct experience and then store the memory of that experience in the human linear mind. For instance, everyone learns that if you touch a hot stove, you will burn your fingers. Children usually learn about this aspect of reality by touching a hot stove and experiencing a burned finger. The fact that hot stoves can burn people is then stored in the linear mind and becomes a memory. The memory of this learned experience is enough to prevent people from getting burned in the future. Although they sometimes have accidents that cause them to get burned, they generally learn to keep their hands away from hot stoves.

People do not learn about hot stoves by memorizing the fact that hot stoves can burn people. They learn about reality through a direct experience which is then stored in the linear mind. However, according to modern education people can learn about reality by memorizing it. Children can learn about electricity by memorizing facts from a science book. People can find out about what the world looks like by memorizing their geography texts. People can learn to appreciate art by memorizing the names and paintings of the "great artists."

People cannot actually learn about life this way. Trying to learn about life through the linear mind is like trying to hit a golf ball with an elephant. The mind was not designed to be used in this way, any more than an elephant was designed to be a golf club. In fact, the mind cannot discover reality. All it can do is read reality in reverse and then supply misinformation about that reality.

The linear mind not only functions in reverse, it also has many other limitations. For instance, it has no way of validating the information that it stores. This means that you can feed the linear mind all kinds of information and misinformation because its only function is to store data. You could tell the linear mind that bicycles burn people just like hot stoves. Without direct experience the mind memorizes this as fact, as easily as it memorizes that hot stoves can burn people. The only thing that prevents the mind from storing incorrect data is direct experience.

Schools prohibit students from accumulating direct experiences by keeping them locked up in classrooms, isolated from the realities of the physical world. Educators can then feed children volumes of information and misinformation which the students automatically store without being able to validate it in reality.

The linear mind also has no self-correction system. Once a piece of information is stored, the mind cannot correct or update that information on its own. Most information memorized by children today will be inaccurate in five or ten years. Many children of the 1950s memorized information about Russia that is very different from the Soviet Union of today. These people now respond to the Soviet Union and the Soviet people based on what they memorized in the 1950s. Similarly, if children memorize the fact that there are nine planets in the solar system today, that "fact" could easily change with the invention of a more powerful telescope.

Reality is always changing. It is not frozen as educators would have people believe. Educators refuse to see that this is a changing universe. Memorizing almost anything, except math tables and a few other things, is completely useless. It would be useful for children to learn how to look up the information they might want to know at any given time. It would be helpful to teach children how to use reference books and how to research certain data. Education, of course, refuses to provide any such skills.

Another way that you can understand this aspect of the mind is to think of a time when you returned to your old childhood neighborhood after being away for many years. In your mind, the neighborhood was just as you remembered it. However, perhaps in reality the neighborhood had changed dramatically. Maybe there were different roads, different neighbors, and new buildings that you did not expect to find. Maybe there was a new highway running right through your old baseball field and a set of stores in the old empty lot where you and your friends sat and talked. Your mind could only correct its impressions and memories of the past when you were able to have a new experience of that reality.

According to modern education, people should trust and value what they know with their minds rather than what they learn through their experiences. In this system, you could safely return to your old neighborhood and go out into the park to play baseball because your mind knows that this area was a baseball field. Through education, people are taught to trust their minds rather than their experiences, which means that you can go stand in the middle of the highway with your ball and bat and play baseball because your mind says this area is a baseball field.

You might say this would be foolish and that people do not do such things. However, they do. They live dangerous lives based on mental misinformation all the time. People know their lives are stressful. They know they have too much chaos and too many problems. People know they cannot find peace. Unfortunately, they cannot see that they are trying to solve their problems with the very part of themselves which is causing the problem in the first place—their minds. They are all out on the golf courses trying to hit the golf balls with elephants, and they cannot figure out what is going wrong with the golf game.

College education relies completely on the human mind. People say that a college education expands a person's horizons. They think they will gain a larger view of the world and have many more career opportunities. In fact, just the opposite is true. A college education narrows and restricts a person's view. The more a person "specializes" in a particular field of study, the narrower his or her vision becomes.

A college education causes people to grow very rigid. Humanity has mistaken this extreme rigidity for real knowledge. In the process of working toward a college degree, students severely limit their employment possibilities. There are many men and women attending college today who have all the natural skills and abilities to become great carpenters, boatbuilders, electricians, plumbers, welders, or masters of other trades and crafts. However, all of these essential options are given no value once a person has obtained a degree. Someone who has studied to become a teacher, for example, can perceive very few other career avenues. Many people who have not attended college see themselves as having more vocational choices than the college graduates. Their only problem is that the educational system has taught everyone to think they are worthless unless they are willing to endure the meaninglessness of college—where they become extremely narrow and rigid as a substitute for real knowledge. People think it is far better to destroy themselves in college than to become auto mechanics or carpenters, whose visions of reality are much more expanded than any college graduate.

Natural Gifts Destroyed

Education not only causes children to abandon their natural instincts for learning and their natural interests, but it also destroys and misdirects children's natural gifts. Some children, for example, are natural inventors. They are the ones who thrive on making things with their hands, things that are original and useful. They rarely have a chance to blossom because they are usually forced to stop using their hands by the time they reach kindergarten. They are forced to switch over to their minds and abandon their natural desires to make things and invent things in the physical world.

Thomas Edison was a man with many natural gifts. He produced over a thousand patents, more than any other man in American history. He designed the first practical incandescent lamp, a scheme for central lighting and power for homes, an electric locomotive, a phonograph, and batteries for automobiles. He discovered electromagnetic waves and electron tubes. However, he never went to college and he never acquired a degree.

There are many potential great inventors sitting in classrooms all over the world. Education has become so destructive over the last ten years that by the time they finish grammar school they will be too linear to be able to invent anything. Their imaginations will have been destroyed. Their original ideas will have been ignored. The natural sparks of creative genius they were born with will have been completely snuffed out.

There are many people who become engineers based on a true desire to help improve human conditions. They want to produce things and invent things to make people's lives easier, but they cannot. They are filled with memorized, linear data and cannot break out of their linear mental systems. Some have been so reduced by the modern educational system that they can no longer relate to their environments, because even their systems for relating have been destroyed.

Engineering programs are particularly linear and mental. They are some of the worst programs education has to offer. They are perfect for snuffing out any last flickers of imagination and creative genius that might have existed in the people who are attracted to engineering as a profession.

Some children have all the natural gifts to design and build homes and offices. Architectural design was once a gift and a skill based on an inner intuition about shapes and designs that were right for people. The purpose for people with this natural knowledge was to help humanity function properly within those shapes and designs. Frank Lloyd Wright was the last of the great architects. He intuitively knew how to build a home so that the angles and shape of the house itself supported a peaceful inner environment. He tried to pass on what he knew to others—students who wanted to learn what he knew. However, he was unable to do this because education had destroyed any intuitive gifts those men and women had originally possessed. Wright's students knew they could not reach what he had done. Most architects today know there is something wrong with their buildings. They know their work is not right, but they do not and cannot correct it.

There are correct shapes for buildings. The United Nations building is one of the worst designs in the Western world. It is a fracture of a whole shape. It attracts people who do not finish things and cannot get things done. It attracts people who live fractured lives. It is the kind of building you would expect to find after an explosion of darkness onto the physical plane, as was World War II. The United Nations should be one of the most effective and powerful organizations in the world. It should be a center of daily interest and concern for all the citizens of the world. Yet, most people do not even know who the United Nations ambassadors are or what they do every day. The fractured shape of the United Nations building actually sets the tone for the fractured and dispersed activity. This is true for most government buildings, and accounts for the reason that people feel so bad when they have to go to their town hall or registry of motor vehicles. The buildings have a bad feeling to them. The workers are unhappy. And much of the cause of the negative feelings and low morale is due to the incorrect shapes and designs of the buildings. They are designed out of the human mind, void of all imagination and intuition.

Some children have natural gifts for carpentry, boatbuilding, and other forms of woodworking. By forcing children to use their minds instead of their hands, education not only destroys any natural gifts children might have for working with wood, but it also teaches children that carpentry and boatbuilding have no value. Education teaches children to think of these fields as hobbies and crafts, not related to anything of real value or meaning. School systems prevent children from developing these gifts by reserving industrial arts courses for boys who have failed. This eliminates the possibility of any female students developing their woodworking skills. It stops males from seeking industrial arts classes because it would be too humiliating for them to be identified with the group of students who have been labeled as failures. Those students who do end up in industrial arts are so devastated by the time they arrive that they have no resources left to develop any natural skills.

People are constantly complaining that they cannot find competent carpenters to work on their houses, or skilled auto mechanics to repair their cars. They cannot find competent people in these fields because education has developed a perfect system for destroying any natural skills and competence in these areas. The men (and rare women) who do become carpenters and auto mechanics are usually directed into these fields only after education has annihilated them. These people are fortunate to be functioning at all given what schools have done to them. Ironically, it is often the highly educated person, who cannot repair his own car or fix anything in his own home, who complains the most about the lack of competence in the carpenters and auto mechanics.

Some children have great artistic talents. Some are natural painters, sculptors, and photographers. Education destroys their natural gifts by keeping them away from paints, clay, and cameras at the times in their lives when they most need to be using them. They need to use them between six and ten years of age. This is the time when education is busy disconnecting them from reality.

The young would-be artists are often very sensitive children and are extremely vulnerable to being disconnected during these years. They should be using their natural gifts to become further grounded in reality. Instead, they are forced into disconnected mental activities during that period when they are so desperate to ground themselves into physical reality through painting, sculpting, or photographing the world.

By the time they reach adult life, their gifts are either destroyed completely so they are no longer aware of them, or they are so disturbed that they can only produce bizarre, disturbed works. Most art-oriented colleges are filled with disturbed people who once had great gifts. However, now their gifts are no longer grounded in reality so their works are like living psychotic episodes, filled with disturbance and distortion. Causing even worse problems for them are the many other disturbed people who collectively will admire these bizarre works and give them credit that is simply not deserved.

When people lose the connection to their natural instincts, they fail to respond to simple problems within their own environments. For example, people spend one-third of their lives sleeping. Yet, a vast portion of human beings who could easily afford comfortable pillows and mattresses continue to sleep in discomfort. An ordinary mattress only retains its quality for three or four years. Most people keep them indefinitely. Hospitals and nursing homes, where people spend all day and night in bed, are filled with broken mattresses. Many elderly people suffer from open sores which bleed and hurt because they are lying all day on inadequate mattresses.

Once people become educated, they are rendered incapable of responding to such simple life problems as buying good bedding because their natural instincts to correct these situations are destroyed. This is true everywhere. If people could look through their homes with all of their natural instincts present, they would see hundreds of unsolved problems, broken appliances and things that need to be repaired. They would discover how these unrepaired and unsolved problems constantly drain them of their inner resources. Unfortunately, most people are so disconnected from their own natural instinct toward improvement, that even if they discover the problems the most they can do is complain that the problems are not solved.

In general, men have been more extensively damaged by modern education than women. As a result of their exclusion from the poisonous educational system, women are a much greater asset to this planet than men. However, even though they are still excluded from equal choices of educational and career goals, this poisoning has begun to affect women as well. The spreading of this condition began to occur when women entered the corporate structure with the expectation and belief that the corporate ladder was something sacred and worth achieving. The new business-women yuppies are now as destroyed as most men. They are not on an admirable path, unless being poisoned is considered admirable.

Women have made great contributions to humanity throughout human history. Yet, because these contributions are so monumental and widespread, they are simply taken for granted and have not been given recognition. The contributions and inventions of men have received greater acclaim, but women have been spared somewhat from the destructive and toxic effects of modern education.

Human Relationships

When children are forced to abandon their instinctive abilities, they also lose their natural sense of intuition. Intuition and instinct are necessary for people to choose proper marriage partners and friends. Modern education has crippled most people in a way that causes them to choose the wrong friends and even worse marriage partners.

Education teaches people to choose their friends and spouses from the mind and not the heart. By the time people are ready to choose a mate, their minds are stuffed with overidealized pictures of who and what they should marry. Since these pictures are generated out of the human mind and not the heart, they have nothing to do with what a person actually needs in a mate. As stated earlier, mental ideas about anything are almost always the reverse of what is really needed. So when people try to find good marriage relationships with their minds, they never find what they really need. They find the reverse of what they need.

For instance, men who need to marry heavy women are only attracted to very thin women whose lives are set up around maintaining their perfect, size ten figures. Women who need to marry men with simple, uncomplicated approaches to life are only attracted to complicated, polluted college graduates who live in constant mental confusion and chaos. Men who need to marry strong competent women only seek weak, incompetent little-girl-types who do not want to grow up. The men who could benefit by marrying this kind of person are only attracted to high-powered female executives.

Education teaches people to rely solely on their ideas. It teaches people to trust and value only their ideas. As a result, very few people are capable of relating from their hearts. Most people do not even like their spouses. They live in marriage relationships for years with people they cannot even call their friends. Most couples lead very disconnected lives with few common interests. Many married people suffer from loneliness and alienation because they are simply living with the wrong people.

Some people try to solve their distressed relationships with divorce. However, since they are choosing their mates from the mind rather than the heart, most people soon find themselves in another equally incorrect relationship with someone else they do not like and with whom they are not connected.

Strange as it may seem, Ronald and Nancy Reagan are well matched as human relationships go. They have developed the kind of genuine friendship and partnership for which most people hunger. The American people have been more forgiving of Mr. Reagan's blunders because they like the feeling of being close to a good marriage, although most people are not conscious of how desperate they are for this. People like seeing the Reagans together. Their relationship is their real legacy to the American people, though people will not necessarily think of things this way.

Education forces students to abandon their own goals, interests, and feelings. By the time children graduate from grammar school they do not know who they are, and because of this they cannot share their ideas, interests, or feelings with another person. So, even if people could choose their partners properly, which they cannot, education would make it impossible to relate to another person in any meaningful way. People are strangers to one another because they are strangers to themselves.

Teachers never talk to students about finding and choosing a proper mate. Teachers never talk to students about how difficult it can be to live with another person or to try to get along in a family. Classroom rules prevent students from talking and relating to one another in school. Listening to teachers lecture all day does not teach children anything about how to relate in the real world.

Teachers never talk to students about how disappointing relationships can be, or about how people always expect too much of one another. Teachers never talk about how painful it is to lose someone you love. They never let students talk about how it feels when someone they have been dating for a long time decides to date someone else, or just drops them completely. They never let students talk about anything that would lead them to relate from their hearts. In fact, most schools punish students for talking during class or for chatting in the halls. Everything in the system is designed to stop healthy relating. By the time students graduate from high school they do not even know what a good relationship would look like or feel like.

Givers and Receivers

There are many natural aspects of human relating that account for healthy, dynamic relationships. One such aspect is that of the giver personalities and the receiver personalities. Human beings are by nature either givers or receivers. Being a giver or a receiver has nothing to do with a person's age, sex, beliefs, or profession. It has much more to do with the way a person naturally functions within his or her environment. In simple terms, receivers naturally receive from their environments, while givers naturally give to their environments.

If people were living by natural instinct and intuition, givers and receivers would naturally mate with one another. Givers and receivers are like magnetic poles that attract one another. The magnetic field between the poles becomes the dynamic give and take necessary for a healthy relationship.

However, people are living by their minds and not their instincts, so everything is turned backward. Givers are attracted to other givers. Receivers are attracted to other receivers. The resulting relationships are lifeless and dead. People know that something is wrong or missing but they just do not know what it is.

Some people who read this information will think they know for sure that they are givers. Others will be certain they are receivers. They will probably be wrong. If you are absolutely certain you are a giver then you actually are probably a receiver, and vice versa, because that is the way the mind works.

When all is going well, receivers in any environment must be certain that the givers are properly cared for so that the giver is nurtured by the act of giving. Receivers must be responsible for making sure the givers are appreciated, and that their natural tendencies toward giving are not misused.

Givers, on the other hand, must be responsible for what they give and to whom they give it. They must be certain that the people they are giving to are people who deserve their efforts. When givers and receivers are responsible in these ways, the relationship then has the foundation for a true friendship.

It should be noted here that human beings are actually not capable of love. Technically, people must have evolved to the level of at least a third degree initiate before they are able to open their hearts. The best that most people can do is find friendship in their relationships. Most people would experience friendship as love. Unfortunately, very few people are well enough to be able to find or to be a real friend.

Givers and receivers tend to experience very different primary emotions. Givers tend to feel angry and hurt. Receivers tend to feel fear. Often in the same situation, a giver will respond with anger and hurt while the receiver responds with fear.

There are many natural distinctions between givers and receivers. There are many other aspects to human relationships in general. People are unable to uncover this kind of information for themselves because they are so disconnected from their instincts that they cannot get at the data they need. Most readers cannot even use this information because they cannot return to the intuitive, instinctive parts of themselves which they abandoned so long ago.

Reader's Quiz

1. *What college did Thomas Edison attend?* _____

2. *Susan B. Anthony received her college degree from which educational institution?* _____

3. *What college did Henry Ford attend?* _____

4. *From what university did George Washington graduate?* _____

5. *Where did Harriet Tubman go to college?* _____

6. *What college did Benjamin Franklin attend?* _____

7. *Alexander Graham Bell graduated from which university?* _____

8. *Where did Betsy Ross attend college before taking her place in history?* _____

9. *Where did Abraham Lincoln get his Ph.D.?* _____

10. *From which university did the Wright brothers graduate?* _____

11. *How could any of these people have a place in history without a college degree?* _____

12. *How could anyone possibly be responsible for changing the course of humanity without a college education?* _____

7

WHAT IS TAUGHT AND WHY

NOTE: This is a book about reality. Reality is not positive. Reality is extremely negative.

IN TODAY'S EDUCATIONAL system only human memory is valued. Educators have completely substituted the idea of developing a good memory for the reality of developing a good mind. Having a good memory is one of many possible mental gifts. Memory is probably the least useful of the possible human mental gifts. It cannot be used to reason, create, imagine, invent, make a decision, or solve a problem. Since education only teaches children to memorize, it does not allow them to develop and use other mental gifts which are far more valuable and useful.

If educators actually understood reality, they would not spend their resources on students simply because the students can memorize. If educators looked more closely, they would see that the students with good memories are not the people who grow up and make contributions to society. They are the ones who are most likely to use what they know to pillage and abuse their own societies.

People with good memories are greedy for information. They are the ones who strive to gain information and compete to obtain the most information. It is bad enough that the data they compete for has little inherent value, but even more damaging is the fact that these students want to hoard information once they obtain it. Schools are set up only for people who want to hoard data. Tests give the information hoarders a chance to demonstrate who has stockpiled the most information in the best way. These students also learn to collect information only for their own personal use. Schools do not teach them to share what they have memorized with their fellow students who are "less gifted." Nor do schools encourage them to go back and share that information with children in lower grades who might benefit from their help.

DATA HOARDING

Very few of the students with good memories have what We call a world view. This means that only a handful of these "gifted" children look out at the world and see many problems to be solved and many people in need of help. Most of these students cannot see beyond the end of their own noses. They spend their high school days waiting for college and graduate school so they can compete for more information to stockpile and use for their own personal gain. They are the ones who are aware that information can be used to manipulate people. Their memorization skills allow them to capitalize on others without ever expressing that information back to the planet in any significant way.

These students are the ones who own the honor societies. They are told that they have these "special gifts" and grow up assuming they have the right to go out into the world and rob their own society. They are the people who go on to destroy the American manufacturing base while they drive the stock market up to dangerously high levels. They are the same kinds of people who drove the market up in the 1920s, and eventually caused the Great Depression by destroying the American economy for their own personal gain.

All subjects now being offered in schools involve the use of memory. Any students who cannot memorize cannot succeed in school, regardless of how hard they try or how gifted they might be. If a child does not possess a good memory, there is nothing for him to do in school. Teachers cannot afford to spend their resources on students who cannot memorize. The few teachers who do try to help these students soon become frustrated and burned out, because children who do not have good memories simply cannot do schoolwork. Teachers who try to help these students begin to feel like failures as teachers. They see that their students cannot do the work in the way the system demands. Most teachers quickly learn that to look successful they must cater only to the students with good memories, and to no one else.

Yet, students with the skillful memories do not grow up and serve humanity. They do not become policemen, firemen, garbage collectors, carpenters, and welders. They become the doctors, lawyers, and politicians. Educators believe that only the potential doctors, lawyers, and politicians are worthy of their efforts. Teachers pretend that these are the ones who contribute to the world.

This is completely backward. For example, garbage collectors are far more important to any society than lawyers, and they are far more dedicated to serving people. When the garbage collectors go on strike, people find out just how important they really are—as any metropolitan resident knows who has lived through a garbage workers' strike.

It is interesting to note that even physicians are less vital than garbage collectors. When the physicians went on strike in England, the death rate decreased dramatically. People became more careful because they knew they had to be more responsible for themselves. While the doctors' strike in Britain made people more careful, the garbage collectors' strikes in the northeastern United States have brought cities to their knees.

It is true that a few people would be burdened or even endangered by a doctor's strike, but many more people would be endangered by a police or fire department strike. Hardly anyone would notice a lawyers' strike, and even fewer would be affected by a politicians' strike. So, who are the most valuable people in society? Who deserves the attention and the resources of the school system—the politicians with the skillful memories or the policemen and women who risk their lives every day? Who is more important—the lawyers with the good memories, or the firemen and women who risk their lives every day? Modern education is the greatest misuse of resources in the history of the human race, and that is a very long history.

Discipline Problems and Emotionally-Disturbed Students

All subjects now taught in schools are presented in a way that involves the use of memory. This includes even those subjects that were once taught without memorization, such as certain aspects of math and science. Textbooks are organized so that a student reads a chapter and then must answer questions following each chapter that are directly related to how much he or she has been able to memorize. These questions have nothing to do with how much the student has learned, or what she understands about her reading.

Students who cannot memorize are perceived and diagnosed as failures. These "failures" may have actually learned more from the chapter, and understood more of what they read than the students who were busily committing their reading to memory.

In some cases, students who cannot memorize are labeled "discipline problems" and "emotionally disturbed." Students with these so-called discipline problems are completely bored in school because schools offer them nothing useful or meaningful to do for five or six hours a day. Teachers expect them to sit still in class, without feeling upset, while they watch the students with memory gifts succeed. In reality, the students with good memories are destroying themselves, but no one perceives the situation in this way. When the "discipline" problems are unable to sit still and feel like failures without reacting, school officials call in the students' parents. They all begin to police the students and punish them in an attempt to make them sit still and fail quietly.

This system always fails. In fact, the "discipline" problems always get worse. Some are able to break away from this travesty by dropping out of school. Others are not so fortunate and stay to graduate before they can find relief.

In inner-city schools, students look upon their classrooms as battlefields. They see school as the only place on the planet where people work very hard at something that is not going to get them anywhere. Inner-city students are poignantly aware of what it feels like not to get anywhere. Many are trapped at home in inferior housing with people who do not have the resources to take care of them. To be forced to go to school, where they will be diagnosed as discipline problems and failures because they cannot or will not memorize, is just too much. When students come to school armed with knives and guns, there is something wrong with what is going on in school. When police must patrol the corridors of high schools, there is something wrong with the educational system. It is not the students.

Other students who cannot memorize, or just simply refuse to destroy themselves, are labeled emotionally disturbed. Educators and school officials believe that students with good memories do not have emotional problems. They are always shocked to discover that a top student has died of a drug overdose or contemplated suicide. Educators equate emotional disturbance with inability to memorize. They sort out the students with good memories in the first few years and devote themselves only to those students. When the students who cannot or will not memorize react to this atrocity, the educators label them emotionally disturbed. These labels usually stick with students throughout their school careers. When these students move to the next grade, their new teacher has usually heard all about Johnny Smith, the problem student, long before Johnny even gets to class.

Educators and school officials have no ability to actually determine which students may have some emotional difficulties that need attention. And when they happen to discover students with real emotional problems, they use those students to pass along their own damages. These are the students that teachers love to humiliate and embarrass because the students are too damaged to fight back. Teachers do not see that students with good memories are far more likely to have or develop emotional problems. These students are simply more equipped to cover up their problems with good grades and high test scores.

Everyone pretends that school is something different than what is being described here. School administrators set lofty goals and write impressive publications that define the goals and expectations of their school systems. They claim to want to improve student minds, when in reality they destroy minds. Officials say they want to help students become good citizens and contributors to democracy. In reality, most students graduate without knowing the difference between Democrats and Republicans. Students have seldom met the mayor of their own town or, even more rarely, their state and local representatives. Schools claim to want to help students enjoy satisfying lives when in reality they do not even let students find out what they are interested in doing. Schools claim to prepare students for adult life when in reality eighteen-year-olds cannot walk the halls without a pass, or change subjects without a note from their mothers.

Students go to school to memorize information, and to be tested on their ability to retain that information. People can make up any cover up or lie that they wish and schools will still be what they are—bankrupt, dangerous, empty places.

Mathematics

There are a few limited aspects of some subjects that would be valuable to memorize. One example might be multiplication tables, which are used all the time. About ninety-five percent of what students are required to memorize is completely useless information. In some cases it is useless because it has no connection to anything real. Math, for instance, is only useful if it is connected into reality. The same is true for chemistry. When students are required to memorize streams of math formulas that are not related to anything, those formulas act to disconnect them from reality.

If mathematics were taught in a woodworking shop, students would be actively using it in a practical way that would then make math meaningful. If students learned geometry while they were building boats, they would learn about angles, parallelograms, and trapezoids because they would see these shapes in the various boat parts. They would learn geometry as a function of building a boat. Today, most students memorize geometric formulas just long enough to pass their tests, and then forget everything they were taught because the subject has no direct bearing on their lives.

Other forms of mathematics could be taught in courses like celestial navigation and weather prediction. There are mathematical formulas that celestial navigators and meteorologists must understand or they simply cannot navigate or predict the weather. Celestial navigation should be a required school subject. People who know how to navigate at sea know a lot about how to navigate in life. They quickly learn that close attention must be given to where you are and where you are going; otherwise you can end up in great difficulty. They usually develop a certain amount of vigilance or awareness of where they are going in life, which is extremely useful both in the human world and in the process of spiritual evolution.

It would also be helpful for students to know something about the weather. This does not mean they should memorize facts about the weather from their science books. We are referring to the real weather that is taking place around them all the time. In today's high tech societies, it is very easy for people to rely on someone else's forecasts and meteorological expertise. Relying on someone else for weather that belongs to you personally is like going out and buying a boat and then telling people that you built the boat yourself. It registers in the human consciousness in exactly this way.

If students were taught about math in reference to their own weather, numbers would mean a great deal more to them. And they would be continuously connected into the physical reality which surrounds them every day. People who pay attention to the weather become more aware of how change affects their lives. They learn that unexpected storms can come through a person's life and cause changes that he or she may not be prepared to accept.

There are other subjects that students could use if the information were grounded into reality and made relevant. There are still others that have no relevance to life at all, such as history and science. There are subjects that should be taught by accomplished masters, such as music, art, and woodworking. At the present time even these subjects are learned through memorization. They are taught by incompetent people who could not get jobs as musicians or artists, so they became teachers because these were the only jobs available. These teachers usually resent their jobs, their incompetency, and their students—which makes learning impossible for even their most well-intended students.

Modern education fails to offer subjects that promote inventiveness or imagination in students. It fails to promote good reasoning and decision-making ability. The system itself is so unreasonable, impractical, and illogical that it destroys reasoning abilities in children who come in with such gifts. The system disconnects people so far away from reality that they cannot make good decisions. They are simply operating on too much inaccurate data.

History

History is a perfect example of a useless subject, which is what makes it so difficult and so painful for children to study. For the most part, history teachers are people who are trying to go backward in life instead of forward. They are people who are trying to go backward to correct their own misdeeds of the past, often committed in past lives long ago. As souls, they fail to see that by going forward they will be given many opportunities to correct their past errors, in ways that will be both productive and useful. As a result of trying to go back to correct their misdeeds, they end up committing even greater crimes by inflicting their own misguided ideas about the past onto vulnerable students in the classroom.

History is the study of ownership. It is the study of who owned what, when they owned it, and what they had to do to keep it. The idea of ownership originated with the British. The English attempted in their own way to colonize the world. Whenever any country attempts to own another, every country reacts defensively in an attempt to protect its own territory. It is like having one child in the neighborhood who goes around taking other children's toys. Soon the whole neighborhood becomes territorial. Children hide their toys. They keep their favorite things locked up in closets and garages. They go on alert to protect their own territory. Eventually, they lose sight of how much they like playing with what they have, because they are so busy protecting their own turf.

Nations throughout the world have lost sight of the needs of their own people because they have become so consumed with protecting what they own. The Russians are extremely territorial. They spend vast amounts of their resources protecting their own boundaries rather than responding to the needs of their people. As a result of the 1987 American Embassy bugging, the Russians overheard enough information to discover that the United States is far less imperialistic than they had imagined. They learned that the American government actually has no interest in taking over Russia or any other country, and that the threatening feelings Russians have experienced are mostly conjured out of ideas generated in the 1950s.

The British have had to learn many painful lessons about ownership. The American Revolution was a surprise and a shock to the British government since they wanted to claim ownership of not only American land, but also of American people. The United States Bill of Rights, which was inspired by the Brotherhood, grew out of British oppression of the United States. The Bill of Rights gave humanity the basic idea that people had no right to own one another. It has become the inspiration for many countries throughout the world. In fact, over 150 nations now have their own individual written form of the rights granted each citizen; all actually based on the original Bill of Rights.

If history were accurately called the "study of ownership," students might be able to learn something about ownership—as long as they were not required to memorize anything. If educators want to call it history, then they should focus on something besides ownership. At this time, history books and teachers offer no real information about real people or life in other times because everything is centered around ownership. History is usually taught in terms of the various wars. Wars are always fought over ownership. They are never fought for any other reason or purpose. Wars always have to do with who owns what and how they propose to keep it.

Human relationships are also constructed around ownership. Marriage vows are vows of ownership. Men and women give each other rings as symbols of ownership. This symbol is insidious in that people pretend the rings have something to do with love and friendship. In reality, a married couple would actually be more free if they attached chains to one another's arms and legs. At least then they could become conscious of what they are calling a marriage or relationship.

When people squabble, it is usually concerning ownership. They are fighting about who owns what in the relationship. Parents constantly fight over the ownership of their children. Sometimes people fight over the ownership of property, or ideas, or power in a relationship. In any case, underlying over ninety percent of the conflict and bickering common to most human marriages is the idea of ownership. The intensity of the arguments is usually a function of how territorial one or both parties might be. Everyone is territorial to some degree, but there is great variation among people.

History, as it is taught, does not give people anything they can use. Memorizing facts about who owned what, when they owned it, and how they kept it has no relevance in people's lives, which is why history is so deadly. The people who teach history not only want to go backward, but they also want to own the past—in the same way that people who collect and own antiques want to own the past. Historical societies are made up of people who want to own the past.

As it is currently taught, history has no value. The people who teach the courses are only relaying hearsay information about what happened at another time. Any Vietnam veteran can tell you that unless a teacher fought in the Vietnam War it is not possible for that teacher to communicate an accurate account of the events from those years. The kind of information that is offered as "historical fact" in the classroom would never hold up in a court of law. It is a terrible system for trying to arrive at the truth.

People also have the idea that teaching students about war will help prevent war. In fact, people who like to study about war want more war. They do not want peace. Peace usually occurs for a short time after a significant war. Then a new generation which was not directly affected by the previous war becomes ready to fight. Teaching students about war has not generally deterred people from fighting. Incidentally, people should not always be deterred from fighting because at this time war is the only way of stopping some conditions of abuse, torture, and destruction.

If schools wanted to teach history from a more helpful point of view, they would teach the history of human inventions. Most human inventions such as the radio, penicillin, electricity, the camera, television and computers were all inspired by the Brotherhood. Each of these inventions dramatically altered the course of human history. Each one also served to connect people from all over the world to one another.

To teach children about the history of war is to teach them to view the world as a fractured and disconnected place. Teaching children the history of human inventions, by demonstrating those discoveries and enlisting experts to talk about their origins, would allow students to learn about the world's miracles. However, educators will never consider this because this kind of history would lift children up, and schools function by keeping children down.

Geography

Humanity's understanding of this planet and how it functions is so disturbed that it cannot even be described as primitive. People have no idea what is going on in their own town or the city next door, or the state and region where they are located, or their own country as a whole. People know nothing about their neighboring nations, nor do they perceive the planet as a single functioning unit.

Geography and social studies, as they are presented by modern education, only cause more confusion and misunderstanding.

People need to see that everything and everyone is related to everything else and everyone else. This is not another New Age light and love approach to the universe. We are referring to the fact that the earth itself has a single function and purpose. The earth exists to provide a physical world in which souls can accomplish spiritual evolution. There is no other reason for the earth's existence.

Right now, people are not using the earth for evolution. In fact, they are using it for everything except evolution, which is why the earth is so rapidly being destroyed. People, particularly those in Western societies, want everything to be natural—their food, clothing, and shelter. Yet, they use the earth in unnatural ways every day to accumulate money, power, fame, and notoriety.

Part of the reason why people misuse the planet is that they have no world view. If they had a world view, they would be able to see that as souls they could incarnate into any nation on the planet. They have probably lived in many other places already. The fact that someone is living in the United States in this lifetime does not guarantee that he or she will come back into a developed Western nation in the next lifetime. If people actually understood reality on this planet, they would not let Third World nations remain in starvation and poverty. They would not allow the human suffering which they simply ignore today. They would know it is possible, and even likely, that they will one day be born into such pain themselves. And if they understood reality, they would clearly see that the physical laws of balance will actually drive them into such suffering if they continue to ignore its existence.

To want to contribute to the world, people must be able to put themselves in someone else's shoes. Having a world view requires that an American be able to imagine what it would be like to live in Ethiopia and spend an entire lifetime just trying to survive from meal to meal. It requires that a Russian citizen be able to imagine what it would be like to live in Venezuela and suffer poverty amidst the drug traffic of the Caribbean.

For the most part, people have no such ability. They cannot imagine life in another country because they are only taught about the world in disconnected geography and social studies classes. Some people develop what might be called a town view. They know many of the people and a lot about what is going on in their own town. They look out at life as though the whole planet functioned like their little town. They feel no impetus to change anything on the planet and see no need to come to the aid of anyone outside of the town. People who develop "town views" usually live in relatively untroubled towns, so they think they are living on a relatively untroubled planet.

Some people develop "church views." These people are usually Christians who have constructed their lives out of fantasies of personal salvation. They believe that as long as they go to church, they do not have to do anything about the suffering and pain on the planet. They usually gather with other Christians who hold the same beliefs. When they look out on life, they see the believers and the non-believers. They are certain that the believers will gain eternal reward (no matter how they live their lives) so they are assured by their fantasies that nothing is required of them.

Education helps keep these narrow, distorted, limited ideas in place. It teaches children to believe they can learn about the world from their geography books. Geography is usually taught by men and women who have never been outside the United States, and who themselves hold a town view at best. Most geography teachers cannot verify that the countries they are lecturing about even exist because they have never traveled to them. Most geography teachers learned about geography in college—not in life. They did not go out into the world and help Mother Teresa in India for several months, or venture into South Africa to live in a black township for a few years. They usually have not gone to see any of the mountain ranges that students must memorize, nor have they ever traveled across any of the great deserts. They are not people who have visited Siberia or explored the open lands of Australia. They are offered to students as experts, yet they rarely know anything about homelessness in a neighboring city or medical treatment needed for AIDS victims in their own state.

Educators who have no world view cannot teach a world view. Most geography teachers see the world as fractured segments, as a group of isolated, unrelated nations. They teach children to study a single country without relating its economy, physical geography, political beliefs, or any such aspects to other nearby countries or to the rest of the world. The interrelationships among nations are key to understanding the overall functioning of the planet. Nonetheless, when geography students are finished with their chapters on Europe, they have no idea how France relates to Portugal, or Austria to Spain. They can name all the European countries and their capitals, but they have no idea how those countries function in relationship to one another or to nations outside of Europe.

Education demands that children memorize facts about their own state and country and about other nations. Most of these "facts" are not only situations frozen in time, but also reflect a very small aspect of a state or nation as it currently exists. Children of the 1950s who memorized the fact that Pittsburgh was the center of the steel industry in America would be shocked to see the boarded-up steel mills and long lists of unemployed steelworkers now making up the welfare roles.

The world is a dynamic, changing place. It is supposed to change and develop in different ways over time. Children cannot develop a world view by trying to freeze reality. Even if educators are incapable of teaching a world view, they could at least stop trying to freeze reality. They could at least teach children how to use geography books for reference instead of attempting to turn the children into walking geography texts.

The best way for children to learn about the world is to go out and see it. The best time for people to travel is under the age of twenty-five. Within the present structures of Western society, most people have no chance to change their fixed, cemented ideas about life after the age of twenty-five. When a person goes traveling after this age, he or she tends to look at new and different people and situations from a very limited, pre-set idea of the world. It is as if the whole world looks like South Vernon Street in Oshkosh, Wisconsin, if that is where you lived most of your life. However, before this age, and especially during the adolescent years, people are generally hungry to discover what is going on in the world. There is no better way to find out than to go and see for yourself.

Science and Creativity

When the early Greek thinkers spoke about the scientific method, they were saying that people could learn much more about life if they paid closer attention to what was going on around them. They intended to teach people that by developing their abilities to observe the world, they could learn more about the world. They were also trying to tell people that observation and direct experience are important research tools; and that if people could directly know something through their five senses they could arrive at more accurate conclusions about life.

The early Greeks were speaking to barbarians. The people of this time had extremely limited mental vehicles. They had little control over their lives, and most of them were completely unconscious about what was taking place all around them.

These great thinkers of their time—Socrates, Plato, Aristotle—were not trying to invent a study of life called science. They were simply using their gifts to help a group of simple-minded barbarians become more conscious about life. They were not suggesting that people extract their observations of reality and write them down in books. They were giving encouragement to people so they would connect with reality as it does exist.

Science is the study of everything. If something is about everything then it is not about anything. Science does not exist except in the minds of educators who think that people can learn about life by extracting out reality and studying it. Today's science books disconnect children from reality. By teaching children to believe that studying about reality is the same as knowing what it is, today's science books disconnect children from reality. Science teaches children to believe that studying about electricity in a science book will cause them to know something about electricity in reality. The way to find out about electricity is to wire a real house with real wires, take electrical appliances apart, make a real lamp, change real fuses, and turn on real circuit breakers.

Science teachers lead children to believe they know something about flowers, vegetables, and insects because they have memorized kingdoms, phylums, and scientific names. The way to learn about flowers, vegetables, and insects is to go outside and plant some real seeds. Then watch to learn what it takes to grow real flowers and vegetables, and which real flowers and vegetables the real insects eat.

Science is one of the most disturbing subjects to the human consciousness. Science exists in everything. Therefore, when teachers try to make students extract out what is already present, students become confused and disoriented. It is simply the nature of the human consciousness. Human beings do not want to split away from reality. To the human consciousness, this is a violent act.

The way all teachers, including science teachers, insure this destruction is by not only forcing children to memorize life, but then testing them on each subject and chapter. When the student takes the test and receives a grade, his consciousness becomes convinced that it knows reality. First, science teachers sever the children from reality. Then, to quiet the shock and confusion, they test the students. By this method, they deceive the children into thinking they have learned something real, when in fact they have not.

Science is like creativity. Creativity is everywhere. People are creating things all the time. To try to isolate creativity as a gift or desired trait severs the human consciousness, just like studying science from textbooks does. Isolating creativity requires that people extract out from reality that which already exists.

Like science, creativity is a made-up human illusion. Creativity exists in everything in the world. Bridges, highways, cars, telephone poles, houses, gardens, trailers, skyscrapers, buses, trucks—all are expressions of creativity. People think they have the right and the skills to determine what is creative and what is not. Teachers think they have the right to test and grade children on what the "experts" have decided is creative. This is experienced by the human consciousness as an all-out assault.

Science and creativity are like breathing. They are going on all the time. Creativity is essential to the survival of the human consciousness, just like breathing is essential to the survival of the physical body. Everyone breathes in order to survive. No one would think of passing judgment on how someone was breathing unless there were some oddity or obstruction in the person's breathing pattern. No one would think of grading someone's breathing. Yet, teachers think nothing of grading things that children create. As for the children, they might as well be graded on breathing because that is how it feels to be graded on what they create.

Art

Educators know nothing about real skill and real beauty. They are so busy judging students' creative works that they cannot see beauty or convey it to their students. Most art instructors have little or no real skills. Schools simply refuse to hire competent, skilled people. Consequently, students cannot rise above the mediocre standards set by the system.

Modern education has disconnected people from skill, competence, and real beauty, and has substituted glamour and hype instead. It has replaced real skill and real art with made-up ideas about what makes a painting or sculpture valuable. What is valuable in the art world is determined by agreement of the "experts." Art "experts" are disturbed people who rise to influence in a disturbed system. Out of their own disturbances they decide what is valuable in the world of art.

This same backward system is functioning everywhere on the planet. The ministers are the ones who place the lowest value on people's natural gifts, because they have the lowest ideas about people. The more verbal they are, the lower their ideas are. Most of the fire and brimstone televangelists have some of the worst ideas about people ever found in human history. They use their positions to inflict those ideas on people by making them feel guilty and bad about themselves.

Art "experts" are people who are completely caught up in self-important images and ideas about themselves. For the most part, they are mentally-distressed people. Many have fractures in their consciousness and keep themselves connected to disturbed astral entities. They live in troubled human relationships with great confusion about male and female polarities.

Almost everything of real skill and beauty is devalued by these "experts." Most of society does not agree with what these influential few have declared as valuable. But people write off their own natural reactions to paintings and drawings because they do not want to appear ignorant. Art "experts" prey upon people's fears of being judged ignorant when, in reality, the art "experts" have all their own ignorance projected out onto other people.

The art world is a world of glamour and hype. It is a world of drugs and disturbed relationships. Most people know that this is true. However, education severs people from their own natural instincts in a way that prevents them from saying what they really think and feel. Education forces children to please teachers and others outside of themselves. Because of this disconnection, people lack the inner self-satisfaction to be able to declare that current art is as worthless as it truly is.

As education has increased in peoples' lives—with longer days, year-round schools, and earlier preschool programs—the art world has been overcome with trash. There are few real artists remaining in the world and even fewer who will survive the educational system. Since the increase of education in the 1970s and 80s, people have developed distorted, contrived ideas about art. For instance, there are actually no "art treasures." When people painted or sculpted a work long ago, they were expressing something about their time period that would have a completely different meaning today. Art has meaning for approximately twenty or twenty-five years. Any real art was meant only to be an expression by some soul, and to represent something about that life during a given period of time. The passage of time following that creative effort does not make something sacred. Art is not meant to be consecrated. Age does not equal value except in a very disturbed world.

Vincent van Gogh and others like him are, at best, apprentices. They are beginning painters. Flat pictures are always the rudiments of actual art. They are valued so highly because everything on the planet today is seen backward.

When people pay millions of dollars for paintings, and allow Third World countries to starve, something is seriously wrong. These backward ideas and values cause corporations, banks and others to value things that have no worth. These ideas cause people to live their lives based on some distorted form of snobbery, instead of realizing that they could help alleviate problems of hunger and poverty. If left to run its course, education will soon destroy all the remaining skill, beauty, and perfection on the planet.

The same disturbances have occurred in the music world. Education refuses to help children develop natural musical skills and talents. The few great musicians remaining in educated Western societies have had to go outside the educational system for competent instruction and support.

The music world, like the art world, is full of unbalanced people. From the 1930s and 40s until today, drastic changes have occurred in music that is acclaimed and considered innovative or creative. Rock stars of the 1980s do not have to be talented musicians. They do not even have to be clean. They can be drugged into psychotic episodes, become violent, and completely lose control of themselves—and their audiences will scream and applaud.

People know this is disturbed. They know that ninety-five percent of current rock music is worthless. They can see musicians from the 1950s and even the 60s returning to fill in the vacuum for real music that the "sound" of the 80s has created.

Parents know something is missing in their children's lives. They know their teenagers are confused, as is the music they listen to every day. However, parents do not understand that the disturbed noises their children call music reflect the inner turmoil caused by modern education.

"Art Appreciation" is another ridiculous notion. No one ever learns to appreciate art by taking an art appreciation course. People either like art or they do not. If they like it, they will naturally go out and find it. They will not need a course in art appreciation to discover this about themselves. However, most art today is so inaccessible to the average person (who cannot afford to pay thirty million dollars for a painting to hang in his living room) that even people who like to look at paintings lose their natural appreciation for art.

Literature

Throughout the history of the human race, great writers and poets have expressed their thoughts and feelings through the pen. When such writers as Henry David Thoreau, Mark Twain, William Shakespeare, and Henry Wadsworth Longfellow wrote stories and poetry, they felt or thought something at the time that they believed needed to be expressed. As souls, each had a need to say something about particular points in their own evolution, and they had the skill to say it in writing.

When these men and women wrote, they did not intend for people to memorize their works. They may have intended to communicate a message and they may have wanted or hoped that people could derive something from this message. They may have written in the hope of bringing some enjoyment or pleasure into children's lives. But no great writers wanted their works to be used to torture school children.

Great stories and poems are written from the heart. They are intended for the heart. They are not intended for the human mind. Memorizing novels, essays, poetry, and plays destroys and ruins their intended meanings. The authors themselves did not memorize their works. Lincoln did not memorize the Gettysburg Address. He did not write the Gettysburg Address so that school children 100 years later would be required to memorize it, recite it, and then be tested on it. He did not deliver this speech because he thought it would make a great moment in history. Most school children do not even know why Lincoln said what he did. They know nothing of what his words mean, or why they might have been important to people at that time. The children only know that if they cannot remember Lincoln's speech they will be embarrassed before their classmates and fail their exams.

Thoreau and Longfellow did not memorize their works. They intended for their poems to be stories. All good stories, poetry or prose, contain a specific message. The message is usually something that only has real meaning to a person if he or she reads it at exactly the right time in life, and at no other time. A story that would have great meaning to one soul would have no meaning to another. A story told or read by someone this year would not have the same meaning next year. In fact, by next year the story would probably be meaningless.

All good stories have the potential for creating a certain effect. If the effect is to be absorbed correctly, the story must be read at the right time in a person's life. The effect may be one which helps a person understand his or her particular circumstances at that particular time. It might be one that jolts a person into a whole new point of view, or it may subtly expose the flaws in a person's current thinking. Education ruins any possibility of children gaining any such growth and insights from stories, essays, and poems. The system not only destroys any inherent message that might be received by simply reading a story or poem, but it also interrupts people's natural instincts to read what is timely and relevant to them in their lives.

Most people are not absorbing the right stories and the right effects. When people announce that they read a certain book five times, or that they have seen the same movie ten times, they are usually absorbing the wrong story. The ones they are most attracted to are the ones which are the most familiar. The familiar stories are the ones that reflect a person's damages, with all the accompanying damaged ideas and points of view. The last thing people need to do is spend time verifying their damaged ways of thinking.

None of the great writers wrote to be analyzed or interpreted. As has been previously discussed, analyzing and interpreting another person's creative expression is an attack on any consciousness. When teachers stand before students and dissect someone's writing line by line, the human consciousness of each student experiences this act as though he or she were being torn apart.

Literature professors and poetry teachers are usually very incompetent people whose natural instincts toward self-expression have been completely destroyed by education. In turn, they use the study of literature and poetry to destroy self-expression in their students. They consider themselves the "experts" on any literary piece. As "experts," they claim the right to decide whose interpretations of stories and poems are accurate and whose are not. They then punish any students whose interpretations are not exactly like their own by giving the students low grades on tests. They not only misuse the stories and poems by analyzing them and interpreting them in the first place, but they go on from there to criticize the interpretations of other people. By giving students low grades in literature and poetry classes on tests that specifically ask for the students' interpretation, these teachers are able to snuff out any remaining threads of self-expression in their students. Thus, they do to their students what was once done to them.

Reasoning and Decision-Making

Modern education places no value on reasoning or decision-making skills. It values only memory—as evidenced by the school curriculum. Education assumes that people with good memories become good citizens who are qualified to do many "important" jobs. Although people with memories are the most successful students in school, they are not generally the most successful human beings. In fact, thanks to modern education, people with good memories generally become very destructive, disconnected people. They usually live extremely self-centered lives. They rarely know how to cooperate with others or how to form healthy relationships.

People with good memories are not the constructive members of any society. They are not the builders or carpenters who make things which contribute to the world. They are not the plumbers and electricians who supply services and conveniences that people need and use in their daily lives. They are not the farmers who supply the food, or the auto workers who make the cars.

People with good memories are the physicians, lawyers, and corporate executives. The would-be physicians today need only ambition and a good memory to qualify for medical school. They do not need to know anything about getting along with people or serving the human race. They are not asked to demonstrate any reasoning ability or decision-making skills, even though they must make critical decisions each day (often under extreme duress) that dramatically affect people's lives.

Physicians today are completely disconnected from medicine's original intention. They have no experience of personal reward and satisfaction for having helped someone in need. They are angry at what they have had to endure in medical school training. They resent their patients because they are not getting any satisfaction from what they are doing. They punish their patients with high fees and think nothing of burdening people with these costs when they are already suffering and in pain. They are interested in their country club memberships, prestigious vacations, and stock portfolios. Their patients fight back with more and more malpractice suits, and insurance rates rise. But no one sees that memory is not enough to make a good physician with a satisfying life.

Physicians have no connection to reality. They cannot understand that it does no good to consume resources by removing a man's heart and replacing it with a new one to allow that man to continue leading a meaningless life. To replace a human heart with another human heart does incredible damage to both people. The person who has died becomes tied in to the physical world so that he cannot get free. After the heart has been removed, the person looks like he has a huge, turbulent, magnetic donut in the area which was once the heart chakra. It takes seventy-five to a hundred years of work in the Inner World to repair the damage to both people involved.

If doctors could see what they were doing in the way We can see, they would stop because they would know these procedures are wrong. Medical practices of the 1980s and 1990s will go down in human history as the most horrendous outcroppings of backward ideas known to man—ideas which could only have come out of highly educated minds with no connection to reality.

The same thing is true for lawyers. Would-be lawyers need only have good memories to gain entrance into some of the most prestigious law schools. It is not necessary that would-be lawyers demonstrate any ability to relate to people or to live by any code of ethics. Lawyers need not have character or be concerned at all with helping people solve their problems.

If everything were functioning in a natural way, lawyers in any society would be the people who insure cause and effect. They are actually the ones designated to help humanity establish values and ethics that come from the continuous re-establishment of cause and effect. However, as a result of the standards set by the modern educational system, eighty percent of the men and women who practice law in today's Western societies are corrupt and dishonest, and place no value on the law. Seventy-five years ago only forty percent of the lawyers were corrupt. As the influence of education has increased, so has the corruption in the legal profession.

Lawyers, like physicians, believe that society owes them the prestige and money they gain in their profession, because they survived the grueling ordeal of law school. When people come to them in times of personal stress, lawyers see them as potential prey. Many people do not need legal advice when they seek it. They need comfort and someone to help them sort out their problems. Those who do need legal advice are usually trying to reinstate cause and effect in their lives—which never happens because the legal system itself is so disconnected from reality. Lawyers believe it is their right to take money from people in distress and to take advantage of frightened people in need of help. Lawyers, like physicians, believe they are superior to others and can therefore treat people as they please. They believe they are superior because education has acclaimed them as successful students—the best the system has to offer.

People who become physicians and lawyers are usually the ones who were the most "successful" students in school. Inside, they feel like they have been raped by the educational system. This is true. They have been raped. However, they have also concluded that this fact gives them the right to abuse others.

When people go to doctors and lawyers, they feel like they are being raped. People can feel that most doctors and lawyers are primarily interested in their clients' money. They can feel that their physicians and lawyers have no real interest in them.

As a result, when doctors and lawyers make errors—even legitimate errors—people are quick to seek malpractice suits. People do not want to be abused. It causes them to want to hurt someone in return. Malpractice suits almost always arise from the feeling that the lawyer or doctor has raped the client—a feeling that the client has actually experienced long before the error that instigates the malpractice suit has even been committed.

8

SYMPTOMS OF A DISTURBED SOCIETY

NOTE: This is a book about reality. Reality is not positive. Reality is extremely negative.

A SOCIETY WHICH places value on the educational system as it currently exists is a society in great danger. As far back as ancient Greece and Rome, people concluded that an educated society was an advancing society. Yet, throughout history, every society has fallen into decline when it invested in educational systems that pushed people into the mental world rather than rooting them into the physical world. Any society which has destroyed its own people's abilities to rebuild should destruction occur has paved the way for its own downfall.

When every citizen is forced by law to attend school, there is something wrong with both the laws and the schools. When children are literally forced to attend schools that destroy all their natural abilities, there is something wrong with the society's value system. America's value system is so corrupt and so incorrect that everything coming from it is incorrect. Even the most well-meaning acts produce negative results, as can be seen in the increased American drug problems since Nancy Reagan began her "Say No" campaign.

Children learn to become content, satisfied adults by interacting every day with content, satisfied parents. There was a time when children did spend their days with parents, doing things and making things together. There was a time when children were a natural part of the parents' workplaces. But this is no longer true. Today children are isolated from their parents for most of the day. They cannot possibly bridge the gap between what they are doing in the classroom and what their parents are doing in the world. It is impossible for them to interact with satisified parents in ways that will produce their own satisfaction with work as adults. As a result, very few children today will grow up to find fulfilling adult lives.

Americans have learned to value only academic and financial success, and to turn away from placing any value on the quality of human life. It is as though there is a place in the world only for people with memory. There is no value placed on skilled laborers who make the cars, or welders who build the bridges. Instead, success, glamour, and excitement have value.

There are people in the world who still speak about the coming of the Maitreya, a great spiritual leader. If such a leader were to come, people would want to stand in line to meet him. There is a group of people who are actually completely preoccupied with the idea of meeting this Maitreya. Their preoccupation makes them unable to comprehend that such a spiritual leader could not possibly come into a world which functions on such a disturbed value system. These people are so fixated on the Maitreya's arrival that they are expending all their own spiritual resources waiting to be first in line instead of doing something about making the world a place where such spiritual help could actually be received.

Education has taught humanity to see the world as a place of "haves" and "have nots." If you have a good memory and have achieved financial success, then you owe nothing to the "have nots." You can take from them as you please and give nothing in return. Even though Nancy Reagan's intentions are good, her "Say No" campaign has failed because it is based on the belief that everyone should be successful as measured by education's standards. This is an extremely disturbed idea. The "haves" cannot demand as much as they do from the "have nots" and then expect them to listen to such directives as "say no" to drugs.

The "haves" feel that they have earned the right to live as they please because they survived—though not without damage—the grueling experience of going to school. Most of the "haves" endured four or more years of college, giving them the right to earn large incomes at anyone's expense and to achieve success regardless of who they must step on to do so. Perfect examples of this can be found among physicians and lawyers. Physicians feel they have earned the right to charge high fees and mistreat patients because they endured and completed medical school. Lawyers also feel that their attendance and completion of law school has given them the right to their country club memberships and stock portfolios.

If you have any doubts about what has been said so far regarding the disturbances in American values, you are encouraged to take the following test:

Readers Test

1. *Do you believe that Mother Teresa is doing good and necessary work?* _____

2. *If you answered 'yes' to Question One, how much money did you send to Mother Teresa last year?* _____

3. *How much money did you spend on makeup?* _____

4. *How much did you spend on your wardrobe?* _____

5. *How much did you spend on jewelry?* _____

6. *How much did you spend on alcohol?* _____

7. *How much money did you spend on marijuana, cocaine, or other illegal drugs?* _____

8. *How much money did you spend on hair styling and hair care products?* _____

9. *How much did you spend on vacations?* _____

10. *How much did you invest in the stock market?* _____

Values and Character

Modern education pretends to instill values and build character in children. Education assumes that values can be established through the mind and that character can be built through memory. People actually establish their value systems over time by imitating the values and ethics of the significant adults in their environments, and by absorbing cultural norms through direct experience.

Children absorb the value systems of their parents, their teachers, and other significant adults. If parents tell their children to be honest but do not live honest lives themselves, their children will observe and absorb the parents' dishonesty. The same thing is true in school. When teachers give children lectures about honesty and other values, these lectures are meaningless. When that same teacher humiliates a child in front of the class for forgetting his homework, children readily absorb the idea that it is completely acceptable for the powerful to prey upon the weak to enhance their own feelings of self-importance and domination.

What children learn in school is to value their minds over their hearts. If they have good memories they learn to develop pride, and begin to see themselves as superior to people without this skill. In the most extreme cases, they develop a kind of academic elitism and join clubs like Mensa for people with high I.Q. scores. They develop such extreme pride in their memorization abilities that they become totally oriented in the mental world. Consequently, they are without friends and family, living instead on the feelings of their superiority over other people. Children who do not have good memories develop deep feelings of personal failure and despair. They, too, have been taught to value only the mind. Since they have not been academically successful, they see themselves as inferior to the rest of society—a view that never changes.

Education also teaches children to value economic success above everything else. It teaches children that getting ahead is more important than being a decent human being; that getting to the top of the ladder is all that counts, no matter who you have to step on to get there. Children learn to believe that classroom life is reality, and that whatever people are doing to one another in the classroom is the way to treat others throughout life.

During their school years children are taught to disconnect from reality, and not to observe or regard the physical world. They are forced to root themselves so completely in the mental world that they disconnect themselves from the real life going on all around them. They lose sight of how their behavior affects other people, and how they need to care for their environments. As a result, most students graduate from high school with very little regard for people and property.

Parents can attest to the fact that this is true. Parents wonder why their children seem so irresponsible toward their friends. They wonder why their children wreck their own bedrooms and seem to care so little about their homes or even their own personal property. What parents do not perceive is that modern education has disconnected the children from reality to such a degree that they almost never see what they are really doing. And they do not even care when they do see.

If teachers wanted to instill proper values in children (which generally they do not) they would need to look very closely at what classroom life is telling children about reality. They would have to look at the screaming madness of the schoolyard. They would need to focus on the mental violence inherent in academic competition. They would have to face the destruction all around them in the schools and schoolyards everywhere. Then they would begin to see exactly what they are teaching students to value.

Character, like values and ethics, cannot be built through the human mind, nor can it be built through the "discipline" and regimentation of classroom life. Being locked up in school all day breeds insanity. It does not build character. People do build character through restraint, but not the kind of restraint found in schools.

A person builds character by discovering some aspect of his personality which causes difficulty for himself and others, and then restraining himself from expressing that characteristic. For example, if a basketball player is prone to quick anger and physical aggression on the court, he or she could build personal character by learning to refrain from expressing that anger or physical aggression in hurtful ways. The restraint cannot be momentary but something which the person works on over a period of time. Another example might be a person who tended to be self-centered and self-focused, who began to sincerely work at focusing outward toward the needs of others. Over time, this person could build character by restraining himself or herself from acting selfishly.

Character is always constructed from the act of restraining some aspect of the human ego structure. Most people spend lifetimes learning such restraint. Schools only encourage children to restrain the natural aspects of themselves, including all their natural gifts, interests, feelings, and ideas. This kind of restraint makes people feel chaotic inside. Schools encourage children to express some of the worst aspects of human behavior without regard for other people, including mental and physical aggression, superiority, pride, ambition for power, cheating, lying, manipulating, and self-centeredness.

Glamour

In any society, glamour is a sign that something very important is missing in people's lives. Because glamour itself is so meaning-less, its presence is a sign that what people have come to value has no meaning. Glamour is always a substitute for real beauty, and grows out of extreme purposelessness.

Centuries ago, it was anticipated that humanity would have certain difficulties with glamour. It was clear to the Hierarchy responsible for this planet that people had set their course in a way that would eventually lead to the kinds of meaningless and pur-poseless lives that spawn glamour and all its accouterments. How-ever, the level of difficulty with glamour in society today is much greater than was anticipated for this time in human history. It was expected that humanity would wend its way into meaninglessness over a period of three to five hundred years. Instead, with the influences of modern education and religion, humanity has burst into meaninglessness at a much faster rate.

The glamour itself presents a very serious problem, far more serious than people can perceive. The fact that humanity has es-calated its pace, and severed from reality at such a rapid rate, makes this condition even more dangerous. Whenever a society throws itself off track, it begins to live in ways that are not natural to that society. The Western world now lives in an extremely unnatural way. The planet earth was intended to be used for spiritual growth and evolution. It was intended to be a place where souls could come to work out the various lessons and tasks required to com-plete the seven planetary initiations. No matter what religious fantasy people care to indulge in, or what they want to believe about life, they are still only here on earth for the single purpose of accomplishing spiritual growth.

When people are cut off from the physical world in ways that prevent them from growing, they begin to live meaningless lives that have no purpose. Evolution is a process of discovering and connecting to reality. Education is a process of disregarding and disconnecting from reality. Over the last twenty years, modern education has so successfully disconnected people from reality that people of Western societies have lost all meaning and purpose in living.

Glamour is one unnatural outgrowth of this severing with reality. It has outcropped at such a rapid pace because education has prevented people from discovering real beauty. Glamour is the human substitute for real beauty. Schools teach nothing about real art or craft. Schools refuse to teach children the skills from which real beauty would be produced. Education refuses to allow a child to create anything in the physical world that could teach her about beauty, such as a crafted wooden boat, a bowl turned on a lathe, or a vase spun on a potter's wheel. Education prevents children from going out into the world and discovering the beauty and perfection found in bridges and highways, or the miracle of a tall skyscraper that does not collapse.

When people cannot find real beauty and perfection in the world, they get the idea of perfecting themselves physically instead of spiritually. Hitler had the idea of perfecting a race of Aryan people. That same idea has now infiltrated Western societies. People want to look like thin, white Aryans. Even schools want all children to be Aryans with good memories. This causes people to use up their resources trying to look, act, dress, or feel a certain way. Many parents are now dressing their preschool children in designer clothes and suits. Some of their children look like little executives. They have already learned to place their focus on how they look, rather than on who they are and what they are on this planet to accomplish.

Some preschoolers look like little mannequins. First and second graders are worrying about their earrings and the color of their shoes. This misuse of resources throws children off track very rapidly because it causes them to focus on things that are not real and have no meaning.

Everything that people do creates energy. Thoughts have shape and form. Thoughtforms, especially collective thoughtforms, carry weight. The thoughtforms of glamour are growing each day in the Western world. Glamour is an integral part of the American value system. Glamour is not just a fad, although it includes fads. Fads are simply ideas that do not lead anywhere. Glamour is becoming a way of life that besieges people in department stores, television campaigns, magazines, and other media.

Glamour is such an unnatural thoughtform that it directly affects the earth by causing the earth to tilt out of its natural orbit. When the earth tilts in this way, it naturally attempts to set itself aright. In the earth's attempts to return to a normal state, natural disasters such as earthquakes, tornadoes, tidal waves, and other phenomena become common.

The thoughtform of glamour is so unnatural that it creates a kind of violence. It is a form of mental violence, and humanity cannot yet see its force or its effects. These kinds of thoughtforms have traditionally been the precursors of war. World War II was a result of thoughtforms collected during the 1920s and 30s. During the 1930s, when people were starving, wealth and other resources were misused. The wealthy people of the world did not try to pull America out of its depression, demanding instead that the depressed and starving pull themselves out. These circumstances created all the necessary mental violence to cause World War II, which was only ended by divine intervention.

Today, very violent and disturbed thoughtforms are amassing. These thoughtforms are already being expressed by teenagers who color their hair blue or green, or shave it off altogether. They wear bizarre clothing with chaotic patterns and mismatched colors. Ironically, these young adults think they are rebelling. In reality they are ultra-conformists.

Teenagers who end up looking like this usually come into this lifetime feeling a little fragile. They have usually had past lives of discontinuity, and attract present-life families who breed more of the same feelings. School becomes the straw that breaks the camel's back. These souls need something steady to help them end all those years of disconnection. Being locked up for twelve years, disconnected from reality, is just too much for them.

They conclude that nothing relates to reality and that life has no purpose. They have so completely absorbed their experiences of home and school (which is really conformity to non-reality) that they express this conformity through their clothes and hair styles. The teenagers who dress more normally only do so because they are still able to pretend that school has something to do with reality.

The disturbed thoughtforms of glamour are amassing at a very rapid rate. People do not understand that collective thoughtforms carry energy which directly affects the quality of life on earth. If these thoughtforms continue to accumulate at their current rate, We anticipate some outbreak of turbulence as the planet attempts to rebalance itself. An outbreak could take the form of a natural disaster depending on how these accumulations affect the earth's plates. A nuclear war or accident would also be a natural result of the current disturbances in natural existence.

Gambling

Gambling is one of the lowest forms of human behavior. It is a sign that people have lost contact with reality and it is, like glamour, a symbol of the meaninglessness that has invaded people's lives. It is a natural human instinct to avoid situations in which the odds are stacked against you. It is natural human instinct to seek self-preservation and avoid situations in which you are most likely to lose.

When people gamble, the odds are always stacked against them. When they play the slot machines, the machines are more likely to win. When they play the tables, the dealers are more likely to win. When they buy lottery tickets, their chances of winning are so slim that no one even talks about the odds. So people must completely disconnect from reality in order to gamble. They must overlook the fact that they will most likely lose their investment.

Gambling is lower than alcoholism and prostitution because the odds are not stacked against the alcoholic or the prostitute. When the alcoholic drinks, he knows he can get high, even though the alcohol may be causing him other problems. When the prostitute turns a trick, she knows that she will most likely be paid. She has probably even been paid in advance. The prostitute gets paid and has sex. The alcoholic gets high and numbed out. The gambler gets broke.

Gambling is much harder to shake than alcoholism. It is harder to shake because the gambler has had to disconnect himself or herself from reality to a much greater degree than the alcoholic or the prostitute. Gamblers also get attached to the high and the tensions associated with "getting lucky." This tension and high help to fill the holes in a person's consciousness that have occurred from the meaninglessness of education.

When We speak of gambling, We are not only referring to the betting man or woman who buys lottery tickets, goes to the racetrack, or vacations regularly in Las Vegas and Atlantic City. We are also speaking of the millions of Bingo players who gather each week (sometimes several times a week) at local churches and clubs. It is not accidental that the church clergy, who work so hard at disconnecting people from reality by getting them to invest in religious fantasies, are in the gambling business as a means of raising money. If churches were really helping people as they claim, they would not have to run gambling concessions to raise revenue.

Along with Bingo for the poor, America also has gambling for the rich which occurs every day on Wall Street. There was a time when companies sold stock to raise capital that would be used to get a company started, or to expand some aspect of an existing company. Today, stocks are bought and sold primarily for the movement of the stocks so that the brokers involved can earn large fees. The company owners do not use profits to improve or expand the corporation, but rather to increase their own personal wealth. The companies often go under. The products fail. However, the stockbrokers and owners of certain corporations become very rich.

Stockbrokers do not care about whether stocks rise or fall. They earn their income by moving paper and by convincing people to gamble on certain stocks, even when they know those stocks will fail. Brokers pretend they are not buying and selling at the expense of others. They act as if they are performing a service. In reality, they are the pirates and thieves, the highwaymen and robbers of the New Age.

Investors in this system are gambling. The odds are completely stacked against them. They have fantasies of making it big in the stock market which have nothing to do with the reality of how and why stocks are bought and sold. The entire stock market has been taken over by corrupt brokers who see it as a chance to make money fast, even though it is done completely at someone else's expense. Gambling always makes money for the person running the casino. The stockbrokers are running the casino and the aspiring upwardly mobile investors are emptying their pockets into the market each day. They get high and tense following their stocks. They live on the illusion that they will get lucky. And in the end, many more investors lose at the stock market game than win.

Because people lose when they gamble, gambling is a self-destructive act. However, modern education has so interrupted people's natural instincts, including the instinct toward self-preservation, that gambling has become a completely acceptable pastime in Western societies. People cannot comprehend how dangerous it is for human beings to lose their instinct toward self-preservation. They have no idea how dangerous it is for a society to spend so much of its wealth and resources trying to get lucky or make it big. They cannot imagine the extent to which people must become disconnected from reality in order to accept gambling as a normal way to live and spend their time and money. Gambling's effects on the planet are similar to those created by glamour. Unfortunately, people are so disconnected from reality that they will not even remember what has been said in this book because it will not seem significant.

Pornography

Sex is not a moral issue as religions would have people believe. Sex is a basic human function like eating, breathing, and sleeping. Religions have imposed many rules about sex which have nothing to do with the welfare of the human race. In fact, these rules have harmed humanity much more than they have helped. When people discover that they cannot live by these ridiculous restrictions, they build up many guilty, negative feelings about themselves.

This section about pornography is not an attempt to raise any moral issues about sex or to make up any new rules about when, where, and how people should engage in sex. We have no interest in attempting to control human sexual behavior in the way that religions have tried to take over this natural human function. Our discussion of pornography is really about mental sex. Modern education forces people to become so rooted in the mental world that even sex, which was once a physical act, has become a mental act for many people. Education, combined with religion, has forced people to view sex as something unnatural and unrelated to reality.

In any culture, pornography is a sign that people have fractured themselves away from normal, healthy sex. Pornography is a sign that sex has been fractured off from the mainstream of life and has become something more connected to pictures and mind ideas than to tenderness and warmth. In school, children learn that life can be discovered in books. They learn in geography to study the countries of Europe and to look at pictures in a geography book. Their teachers usually cannot even verify the fact that these countries exist because the teachers themselves have never been there. High schools and colleges do not expect students to go discover Germany, France, or Belgium for themselves. They, too, expect students to study these countries and look at the pictures in textbooks.

When everything is taught through words and pictures, people eventually believe that words and pictures equal reality. So when they study Germany from a book—looking at the pictures and listening to someone lecture about Germany who has never even been there—they start to believe they have had the same experience of Germany as someone who has visited or lived there.

The same thing is true about science. Children believe they are learning about the weather when they see pictures of the sky and various cloud formations in their science books. Educators would not think of setting up their own weather stations, or walking the children outside each day to learn about weather and clouds from reality. Instead, schools force children to memorize terms and look at pictures of clouds, as though reality were in the books and in their minds.

Pornography is sex in mental pictures. It is as real as the pictures of Germany in the geography books, or the clouds in the science books. It is safe, detached, and unemotional. It does not require relating or connecting with anyone, and it is an expected outgrowth of a world in which "reality" is thought to be in words and pictures rather than in the physical world where it actually exists.

Pornography is only a symptom of an even greater sexual problem. Very few people are still connected to their own natural sexual feelings. Over ninety-five percent of the people living in educated Western societies are disconnected from their natural sexual feelings. This disconnection causes people to mate with all the wrong sexual partners and to substitute sexual excitement for real intimacy and warmth.

People who think they have good sexual relationships generally do not. They usually have some form of regular mutual stimulation in which each person is connected to his or her own separate ideas about sex, rather than to the real live person with whom they claim to be making love. Sex leaves most people feeling empty and alienated because it has become such an alienated, mental act.

There is a purpose for sex in the evolution of the human consciousness for some people. However, humanity is so far away from the place where people could begin to use sex as it was intended that it would be ridiculous to even speak about it here. To talk about the proper uses of sex would be like discussing the final coat of varnish on a sailboat with someone who cannot hammer a nail. It will be a long time before humanity understands that the boat even needs to be built.

Drug Problems

Throughout the history of humanity, people have managed to discover substances that could be swallowed, smoked, snorted, or somehow ingested to cause various alterations in the human consciousness. Each society uses alcohol and/or drugs in an attempt to block or numb out the problems specific to that society. For example, in Russia people use drugs primarily to cope with the anger and despair caused by the oppression of normal, healthy, adult life. Russian people look out at life and feel hopeless to better their circumstances or to improve their conditions. In a sense, the Russian people are still responding to the terrorism of the czars and the atrocities of Stalin. Their alcohol and drug abuse allow them to block out the fact that their own government has not yet condemned the devastation caused by Stalin. Their own government still lives in the lie that Stalin was a national hero. Mikhail Gorbachev has started the process of unraveling these historical difficulties. However, there is still much work ahead before the Russian people feel uplifted in any way or sense that they have regained control over their lives.

In some South American nations, people use drugs to block out the pain of poverty and the desperation of human living conditions. People in Chile, Argentina, and Brazil feel the bankruptcy all around them. They feel it in the culture, the government, the misuse of resources. Drugs and alcohol temporarily relieve them from their surrounding nightmares.

In America people use drugs and alcohol primarily to cover up feelings of personal failure. These feelings of failure are a direct result of the educational system at work. This is not to say that people have no other problems contributing to alcoholism and drug abuse, because they do. Nonetheless, the primary reason that Americans turn to drugs and alcohol, particularly at such early ages, is that schools cause them to feel like failures at life before they have even had a chance to live it. American children do not graduate from high school with the feeling that they have something worthwhile to do with their lives. Even "successful" students feel like they have failed at life because they are so incapable of responding to the demands of the real world.

America's drug problems are on the rise. Younger and younger children are seeking drugs as a way of numbing themselves out to the fact that they feel like failures. Drug education is a joke to most children. In some schools children even have to memorize the names of the most popular drugs and the reasons why they should not use them. For many children, drug education becomes their introduction to drug use and abuse.

Drug education has never worked to solve America's drug problems. History can prove this fact. The backward effects of Mrs. Reagan's "Say No" campaign have already been mentioned. Drug reformers cannot display a famous athlete or movie star to people who feel like failures and expect those people to say no to drugs. One in ten of those athletes and actors is actually sincere. The rest are using the campaign to gain notoriety. In either case, the overall effect is just more feelings of personal failure for the drug users.

America's drug problems will only continue to grow as schools proceed to disconnect children from reality at earlier ages. The children are beginning to feel like failures at life much sooner than they once did. In reality, schools have failed children. Schools have failed to help children develop the skills and interests that would cause them to feel they could do something worthwhile with their lives. Schools assume that children have no interest in contributing to society until they become adults. And because schools do not teach children how to contribute to society, they actually prevent children from becoming adults.

At fourteen and fifteen years of age, children naturally want to launch themselves into adult life. In many cultures these are the ages when children are considered adults. It is the time when many "primitive" people mate and have their young. In fact, it is the ideal time for people to carry and bear their children. They have much more energy at fourteen or fifteen through age nineteen to care for infants and small children than they do at thirty or thirty-five, when it is more natural for people to be on to other things.

American children are not prepared for anything when they are fourteen or fifteen. By sixteen at the latest they should be moving into responsible adult life, but modern education has so ill-prepared them that they fail at adulthood and fall back into childhood. Modern education cripples children to such an extent that they have a very difficult time establishing themselves as independent adults and seeing a place for themselves in the world. American teenagers do not have the resources to lift themselves into adult life. They do not have the resources to mate and bear children or to establish any kind of meaningful adult life in the world.

If Americans want to solve their drug problems they must first solve their school problems. They will need to find a way to help children feel worthwhile and successful at life. They will have to give children things to do in school that are worth doing. Then Americans will discover that children who have something worthwhile to do with their lives are far less likely to care about taking drugs.

Care of the Elderly

Parents prepare their children for school by telling them that school is a good place where children can go to learn and have fun. By doing this, parents betray their children. Most children know they have been betrayed by the time they reach second grade. It is a terrible shock when children discover that their parents have lied to them. It is even more devastating to uncover the fact that their parents are aligned with teachers and not with them, except in rare circumstances.

As schools become more achievement-oriented and grounded in the mental world, and parents become more preoccupied with their children's academic success, children feel increasingly betrayed, deceived, and abandoned by the people they love most in the world. This whole experience is now so completely acceptable and institutionalized that children have no recourse. They have no one to talk to about what has happened or how they feel. Their parents are the enemy. The school system is the enemy. The children are too young to fight back.

In the physical world the scales must always be balanced. It is the law. And although it takes fifty or sixty years, the scales do get balanced. When the children grow up and the parents grow old, the parents become vulnerable and turn to their sons and daughters for help. The parents forget that they betrayed their children when they were vulnerable. They sent their young children to places where they did not want to go, to be cared for by people who punished and humiliated them. But the children cannot forget. In fact, they only know how to respond to vulnerability in the way that their parents and teachers have taught them. So when their parents need them the most, they send their parents off to nursing homes to be cared for by people who often do not want to care for them and who humiliate them and punish them.

How many times have you heard children say, "Please do not make me go there," in reference to school? How many times have you heard parents say, "Please do not make me go there," in reference to a nursing home? Many sons and daughters do not want to treat their parents this way, but by physical world laws they must balance the scales. Also, they respond to vulnerability with the only behaviors they have, the ones learned from the parents.

There was a time not too long ago when Americans lived in extended families and expected to care for aging parents and other relatives right at home. Nursing homes and hospitals were only for the very ill. Good home care was common practice. In comparison, very few families today take on the responsibility of caring for aging parents and relatives. Health care for the elderly is steadily declining. Nursing homes are often substandard at best. Elderly people, who can barely tend to themselves, live alone. Some rely on home health care and spend days in bed waiting for a caregiver to come and feed them. Alienation, isolation, and despair are common. And these conditions are not improving. They are not improving because as education becomes more destructive, children feel more betrayed and deceived by their parents. The children harbor resentment toward their parents for sending them to school and leaving them in the hands of abusive teachers. They hold their parents in contempt for siding with teachers and school officials at the times when they most needed their parents' support.

The children's hurt and depth of anger at their parents for sending them to school goes unnoticed. There is no way that any child could directly face the horror of this situation. Children go through their lives thinking that the problem is within them. However, even that does not change the underlying feelings of betrayal that nearly all children in Western society carry toward their parents.

The health care problems and mistreatment of the elderly are an expression of withheld anger and hurt at being so deceived and betrayed. By the time children have grown up they have usually completely forgotten about how they felt in school. However, the anger and hurt have not gone anywhere. Anyone who works in a nursing home can tell you that people generally do not visit or tend to their aging parents. Anyone who has ever worked as a home health care professional can tell you that life conditions for many elderly people are a travesty.

It will be hard for people to see the relationship between the parents' betrayal of their children in early school years and the mistreatment of the parents later in life. The fact that this relationship is difficult for people to comprehend is why the problem has become so widespread and dramatic. Sending a parent off to a substandard nursing home or leaving a parent in an apartment for the elderly is now common practice, just as sending a child off to school is common practice. No one questions the school system and very few question the quality of care being given to the elderly. A quick tour of almost any nursing home in a low or middle income community will clearly demonstrate that the residents of those nursing homes have not been placed there out of love. Spending a day visiting homes of sick, elderly people who live alone in your town will also demonstrate that they are not living this way because someone loves them. The more education destroys children, the more the care of the elderly will deteriorate. One who looks closely while touring a nursing home or visiting the sick and elderly who live alone might conclude that someone is trying to torture these people. Someone is—someone who sat for twelve years in classrooms where children were tortured every day through humiliation and punishment.

The Corporate Law

Corporations are run by educated business executives. They are directed by people who have business school degrees and educated ideas. These people have succeeded in school, but not because they are able to relate to people or because they have good decision-making abilities and reasoning skills. They know nothing about making cars, computers, copy machines, or any of the products produced by the companies they direct. They are successful because they have good memories and the ambition to want power.

Corporations are run by people who believe they have been saved by their religions and are therefore free to live their lives as they please. They are free to amass their own private fortunes, free to make decisions which destroy people's lives, free to seek power, and to enjoy the privileges of the executive lounge. They are free to turn their backs on hunger and homelessness and to spend their time tending to their stock portfolios and country club cocktail hours.

Corporate executives become very alienated people through their religions and through modern education. Very few automobile company executives know how their desk drawers are made or why depressing their brake pedals causes their cars to stop. Very few IBM executives can assemble a computer if given the parts. The Xerox executives cannot repair their own copy machines. These are the same executives who believe they do not have to know anything about people in order to manage them.

There was a time when the people who ran the auto industry knew how to make cars, and the people who ran the computer industry knew how to make computers. However, education—particularly the specialty of business—has changed all that. Today, corporate law dictates that the less you know about the corporate decisions you make, the better off you are. The more you can remain detached and disconnected from the results of your decisions, the more powerful you can become.

It is ludicrous enough to have people running companies who know nothing about those companies, but to allow people to make decisions without holding them responsible for the results is to destroy an economy. Corporations of the 1980s, based on the corporate law of decision-making, run only on the self-interests of the executives in command. If the General Motors' Board of Directors ate breakfast in the homes of the people who work on their production lines, their decisions would be very different. Today people have power, but they are so alienated from their own decisions that they do not experience the results, only the power.

The effects of corporate decisions on the lives of American workers and on the American economy are far worse than people can imagine. Auto workers know that something is wrong when executives vote themselves millions of dollars in bonuses one year and lay off thousands of employees the next. Education has so destroyed people's connections between cause and effect that the executives who have made those decisions still do not see how disturbed they are. The executives cannot see because they still have their jobs and all their power and wealth. Only the auto workers standing in the unemployment lines know what these decisions mean.

Corporate executives, like physicians and lawyers, do not seek their positions in order to gain real satisfaction. They seek them only for power, prestige, and money. As a result, they do not find satisfaction in their work or in their lives. In the 1980s, more and more companies offer "perks." "Perks" are a substitute for real satisfaction and fulfillment in life. The more dissatisfied people become, the more they need perks to compensate for wasting their lives doing something they do not like. The more executives need perks, the more they will grant themselves bonuses. The more bonuses they take, the more laborers will join the ranks of the unemployed. Americans have not yet felt the full impact of the new corporate law of decision-making. If things continue on their present course, people will soon know more of the effects of this system—much more than they would want to know.

We should also note here that many governments run like corporations, and many political leaders live by the corporate law. Most American politicians are not connected to the people they represent. For instance, how many legislators who have written welfare laws over the last ten years have actually talked to a group of welfare recipients to find out about their needs? How many of these lawmakers have even tried to live for one month on the amount of money allotted a welfare family? How many legislators who voted for a 65 m.p.h. speed limit increase did so because they like to drive fast, rather than looking at the reduction in traffic fatalities attributed to the 55 m.p.h. limit? How many of them live near a nuclear power plant? How many of them have ever been faced with a medical emergency and no health insurance? Education has taught them all to believe they are qualified to make laws and decisions that affect people's lives without ever dealing directly with the people. All they have to do is read about health insurance, welfare, or nuclear power, and they are automatically "qualified" to decide on the policies that affect the lives of millions of people.

9

CHILDREARING IN THE AFTERMATH OF DARKNESS

NOTE: This is a book about reality. Reality is not positive. Reality is extremely negative.

ALTHOUGH HUMANITY HAS officially entered a new age of light, the long age of endarkenment has left family systems in complete disarray. Under natural circumstances, parents would have children to learn certain things about themselves that could not be learned another way. Under natural circumstances, parents would learn about themselves through their children's dreams. This means that mothers and fathers would be completely dedicated to helping each child accomplish his or her individual goals and dreams. In this natural system, if a child wanted to become a butcher, both parents would help the child become a butcher, no matter what they thought or felt about that work. If a child wanted to become an economist, both parents would help that child find a place in the field of economics. In the process of helping children fulfill their dreams, parents would be nourished and would gain the learning and resources necessary to promote their own growth as well as the growth of their children.

Unfortunately, darkness has left humanity in a backward state. Instead of trying to help their children fulfill their own dreams, parents do everything possible to make the children fulfill the parents' dreams. Fathers who wanted to become doctors, but could not, influence their children to become doctors for them. Mothers who always wanted to own their own businesses, compel their children to own businesses for them. Over ninety percent of parents in Western societies are completely dedicated to preventing their children from fulfilling their own personal dreams, and are equally dedicated to steering their children into realizing the unfulfilled hopes and fantasies of the parents.

Education plays a vital role in this process. Parents want their children to attend schools that will promote the parents' dreams. When parents move into a new area and go out looking for the "right" school system, they are almost always searching for the school which will help them take over their children's lives so that their children will grow up to fulfill the parents' dreams. Rarely do parents have the intention of finding a school system to meet the needs of the child—one that would help a child follow his or her most natural way.

Teachers are like a collection of parents who have their own unfulfilled dreams. Teachers often have histories of personal failure. They want students to succeed in school as a way of fulfilling those aspects of the teachers' lives where the failures occurred. In this sense, education is a natural outgrowth of completely endarkened childrearing.

Most children resent their parents. They feel pressured to do and be what their parents want them to do and to be. This pressure causes many young adults to move away from their parents because it is the only way they can feel free. People do not move away from people they really love. They move closer to them. Most young adults want to get several hundred miles away from their parents. They want to call their parents once in a while and visit as infrequently as possible. Then they want to claim that they really love their parents, which of course is not true or they would live near their parents and feel like friends. This is not to say that everyone who lives in the same town with his or her parents loves those parents. There are hundreds of pathological reasons for staying with parents or continuing to live nearby. This example is given only to point out the lie people tell themselves when they move as far away as possible from the people they claim to love the most.

These defective parenting practices produce great unhappiness for adults in Western societies, because so many people are doing what their parents want them to do and ignoring their own natural instincts and interests. Most adults know this is true. Very few are truly free.

People who read this will make a serious mistake if they decide to use this information to condemn their parents. There is no one to blame for the legacy of darkness which people find in their lives. In fact, any reader older than twenty-five has, in all likelihood, already nailed someone else exactly the way that you have been nailed by your own parents. If you have children, it is likely they are acting out your dreams. They are probably acting out many of your unfulfilled fantasies, which include not only career dreams but also personal wishes—like being mentally unbalanced, depressed, or drug-dependent. If you do not have children, then your spouse or significant other is probably out fulfilling your dreams right now.

No one is to blame. However, no one is without responsibility. Most young adults and many older adults believe they should condemn their parents as a way of making them see the harm they have caused. People would do much better to simply face the harm they cause every day in their own lives, without trying to shift the focus onto their parents.

Most parents, deep inside, regret what they have done with their children, but they do not know why. They have the feeling they have done something wrong, yet they cannot tell you what it is. These parents cannot recognize their feelings because they have also forgotten the pain of their own early lives and their own misbegotten goals.

Parents want their grown children to live near them. This would allow parents to feel better about what they have done. However, grown children will not let their parents feel better. The children know that the parents have nothing to feel good about but they would never say this aloud. People say just the opposite. They say that they love their parents, while they set up their lives 3,000 miles away and visit once every three years.

People make up a lot of excuses about how they feel toward their parents and how they love them. It is actually natural for people to have bad feelings toward someone who was not in their corner at a time when that was needed and should have been provided. Again, We provide this discussion not to incite people into pouring their hurts onto their parents, but merely to point out how ludicrous it is to pretend to love someone when you really feel betrayed.

The Destruction of Parental Skills

If parents were able to respond to their children's needs correctly, they would never allow children to attend schools as they now exist. Parents would see how vulnerable their children really are and would never place them in the hands of the educational system. They would not allow themselves to betray their children and become part of the cover up that now allows educators and school officials to abuse and destroy children with parental consent.

However, parents are also victims of this system. They are only doing to their children what was once done to them. For parents to help children fulfill their personal dreams without inflicting their own hopes and expectations onto those children, parents must be healthy and fulfilled themselves. Parents must feel satisfied with themselves and with their own lives. They must have enough love in their own lives, and feel nourished and nurtured enough themselves, to be able to tend to children.

Modern education does nothing to prepare students to become good, healthy parents. The reverse is true, since schools destroy the natural instincts and intuition that parents must have to respond properly to the needs of each child. Parents cannot know what their children need by memorizing facts about children and families from books. They cannot learn how to respond to a child by seeing pictures of families on the classroom walls.

In healthy families, people must learn to get along with one another and to share each other's resources. They must learn to support one another's goals and interests. In schools, children are taught to ignore their own goals and interests as well as those of the people around them. They are taught to believe that everyone is the same and that everyone must be interested in the same things. They think all people learn in the same way, at the same rate of speed.

If education were functioning properly, schools would provide children with two things. First, schools would help children discover themselves, and secondly, the outside world. In order for children to discover themselves, they would need to relate in healthy, natural ways with other children. This interaction with other children would allow them to begin to determine who they are and how they fit in the world.

Schools prohibit children from discovering themselves. Children are prevented from relating and interacting with their friends at school. When children try to interact with others they are disciplined, embarrassed, and punished. Since children cannot ever discover themselves in this way, they have no hope of finding out how to relate to another person or how to get along in a family. Any of the natural skills necessary for healthy parenting and family living are destroyed before children even finish grammar school.

Once modern education destroys these natural aspects of the human consciousness, it then fills children with false ideas and fantasies about family life. It is as though educators believe you can teach children about family life by showing them pictures and telling them Dick and Jane stories about how families live. Pictures are flat, linear portrayals which have nothing to do with reality. Teaching children about family life by talking about pictures in a book, or referring to posters on the wall, is like trying to introduce your parents to your fiance by presenting his or her picture and then introducing them to the picture as though it were a real person. If someone actually tried to do this, people would consider that person to be deranged. Yet schools do these deranged things on a daily basis.

Family life cannot be discovered through pictures of slim, white, glamorous parents and their slim, white, glamorous children. People do not learn how to relate to one another and to share life experiences by sitting in a classroom where they are forbidden to relate.

Humanity has few models for healthy parenting and none of those models are seen by children in school. Indeed, the teachers who are the parent figures in children's school lives represent some of the worst adult role models possible. Teachers are the least concerned about the needs of their students and are interested only in their own personal goals and interests. If teachers were interested in students, students would be treated as individual human beings. They would not be statistics on a bell-shaped curve. Even the healthiest people could not emerge from the current educational system with any ability to provide correct parenting or to promote a productive family life.

Spiritual Evolution

To begin to comprehend how disturbed and misguided childrearing has really become, it is necessary that people understand something about spiritual evolution. The first volume in this series, *The Psychology of Spiritual Growth*, is a basic primer for such understanding, should further information be sought. Souls come to this planet in order to grow spiritually and to accomplish the seven planetary initiations. Each soul has his or her own unique way of accomplishing this task. Each soul has different needs, interests, and requirements which is partially why education's "one size fits all" approach is so deadly.

Each soul requires certain responses from people in his or her environment which inspire and stimulate that soul's urge to grow. If everything on this planet were functioning in a natural way, souls would be magnetically drawn to exactly the right parents in any given lifetime. Souls who needed independence and freedom would be drawn to parents who could provide them with independence and freedom. Souls who require continuous reassurance and physical nurturance would be drawn to parents who could provide them with exactly the right kind of reassurance and nurturance. Souls who needed mental stimulation would be drawn to families where people talked about world problems, political views and other things that would mentally stimulate the children. Souls who are looking for quiet and calm would find families who fostered calm environments. In short, each soul would seek and find exactly what was needed in a family environment for that soul to thrive.

However, the era of darkness has left people so damaged that they have lost their natural abilities to attract what they need. Children are magnetically drawn to parents, but rather than finding what they need to grow, they are drawn by their own damages into the damages of the parent. As a result, children end up with the wrong parents lifetime after lifetime, and are unable to correct their own circumstances. Souls who need independence and freedom are drawn to parents who want to control and dominate their children. Children who would be comforted by controlling and dominating parents end up with parents who want independent, freedom-loving children. Souls who require mental stimulation are born into families where nobody talks about anything, while children who need quiet find mentally-stimulating families—which they experience as chaos and confusion.

In Western societies, young souls (those who have spent relatively few lifetimes on the planet) are sometimes born into families with financial resources. Many "preppies" are actually young souls. They are born into these circumstances so that their early incarnations can be protected. As young souls they lack inner depth, which is why they are attracted to one another and to the local yacht clubs and country clubs. Their early lifetimes should be a time for discovery of themselves, just as kindergarten age children naturally discover themselves before education destroys this natural instinct.

However, the young souls now being drawn to these families for protection are also pulled into the false values and ideas of the upper classes. These are the children who are dressed in designer clothes as schoolchildren, and paraded around at debutante balls as teenagers. They are preoccupied with how they look and who they know, rather than with who they are. What should have been helpful early lifetimes have become spiritually deadening. These souls are looking for all the wrong things in all the incorrect places.

Once people are damaged by some trauma or tragedy in the human world, they are rarely able to recover from that damaging situation with only their own resources. The darkness has caused people to misuse their resources so extensively that they cannot focus their energies productively for a long enough time to alleviate the damage. Worse than that, people then begin to attract similarly traumatic situations in which more damage is incurred.

Modern day psychotherapy is a pathetic attempt to help people recover from damage. It is pathetic because the psychotherapists themselves are so destroyed that all they can do is use their clients to pass along their own unresolved hurt and pain. Clients almost always get worse, even when the passage of time has given them the illusion of getting better. The best that any psychotherapist could do under these circumstances is help the client feel that he or she is no longer alone. When children discover that they have been betrayed by their parents because their parents have sent them to school, they feel very alone in the world. If a psychotherapist really likes a client (which is usually not the case) that therapist may be able to convey a feeling to the client that someone is finally in his or her corner. This experience can be extremely positive. Although the damage is not healed or eliminated, the client begins to feel better about himself or herself and about life because he or she is no longer alone. Unfortunately, this positive experience is extremely rare since most therapists have no real concern for their clients, and no idea of how to give such support or service to another person.

The actual healing of damages requires the use of tremendous spiritual resources which are not available to any psychotherapist or New Age spiritual type. What these people have are ideas, not healing abilities. Most of these ideas are incorrect and do not lead anywhere. The few New Agers who do have the right idea are too mentally destroyed, usually by education, to do anything about what they know.

To further complicate matters, souls also collect incorrect, inaccurate ideas throughout their lifetimes. These ideas come from decisions made in times of trauma and distress. Those decisions and the resulting incorrect ideas are actually stored in the soul, and are therefore not relinquished at physical death. Because these ideas resulted from decisions made during trauma and turmoil, they have nothing to do with a person's current reality. Yet, many souls do not easily relinquish these ideas, even when they are encouraged to do so in the Inner World between incarnations. They are just unable to see that their conclusions and ideas about life are not true in reality.

The notion of souls harboring incorrect ideas is difficult for most people to understand. Most religions teach people to think that souls are somehow infallible because they are the part of a person which is like God. The Monad, the spiritual part of each person that directs the soul to fulfill its requirements, is actually the part of a person that is like God. The Monad is the cause of the person's existence and can guide and direct the soul if damages or incorrect ideas are not in the way.

The incorrect ideas carried in the soul also draw people into the wrong families. Some souls who need nurturance avoid nurturing families because they came to the conclusion during a traumatic event that they must be self-sufficient or they will die. Some souls who need regular physical comfort avoid families who give physical comfort because they came to the conclusion during lifetimes of physical abuse that all physical contact causes pain. Each individual soul has unique needs. What makes current reality so painful for both parents and children is that so few people are correctly matched. If all the children on earth would randomly select a new set of parents, this random selection would result in more properly matched families than anything the current system can provide. It is estimated that such random switching would cause relief in up to half the families on the planet. It would not eliminate damage but it would eliminate some pain because half of the parents and children would no longer be aggravating each other's weak points and old wounds.

The Role of the Parent in Society

Most parents base their decisions to have children on their own damages or their fantasies about children. The era of darkness has left humanity in such disarray that people rarely decide to have children from their natural instincts to do what is right for themselves. Between past-life damages and modern education, people have no natural instincts left. Natural instincts refer to those aspects of a person which lead him to do the things that are spiritually correct for himself. The spiritual way is always the natural way.

Because people can no longer find the natural way or the spiritual way, most people end up wasting their lives doing all the wrong things. The fact has already been mentioned that people who need to spend their lives farming attract none of the cues or life situations to lead them into farming. Part of the reason so many farms are now failing is because the people doing the farming belong in other careers. This fact, however, does not overlook the economic burdens placed upon farmers, and the disrespect and disregard for farming that stems from modern education. These external circumstances are obviously contributing factors to the failing American farms.

However, farming as a profession takes a very specific kind of person with a very specific need to connect into the physical universe through the land. Real farmers are people who cannot get close enough to the soil, the crops, and anything else that would root them, in ways required by their particular system, into physical reality. The few farmers who do seem to be withstanding the difficulties of the time are usually the ones who belong on the land. Their attitude is that they will remain "come hell or high water." This attitude is a function of that farmer doing what is most natural and correct for himself or herself spiritually.

The same thing is true about parenting. Parenting is a vital role in society. It is probably the single most important role. Like farming, parenting is assigned no value and commands no respect. People have much more respect for the stockbrokers, who are destroying the American economy, than they do for the farmers who are supplying them with food. People have much more respect for corporate executives, who cannot fix a leaky toilet, than for parents who are responsible for a whole new generation of souls.

Because everything is so backward, people who would make very good parents are not the ones having the children. This is not true in every case, but it is true more often than most people would like to think. Many of the childless or one-child "yuppies" of today are people who have the emotional, economic, and spiritual resources to properly parent children. However, programmed by modern education, they are directing all their resources and energies into earning high salaries and living "successful" lives, even if they do have children. They are exactly the ones who have something children need. But thanks to modern education, these people are too busy being successful to want to give anything of themselves to children. It has become an "in" thing not to have children, or not to let children interfere with one's career needs. The people who are responding to this "in" idea are exactly the ones who could help turn the improper parenting cycles around.

Conversely, many of the people who are having children do not have the resources to care for them. In the most extreme example, the poorest countries in the world are the ones bearing the most children per mother. They are the countries where the people are the least equipped to have and to raise children correctly.

Even in developed Western societies, many of the people who become parents do not have the interest or the resources to raise healthy families. Many parents are just too damaged themselves to be able to care for another person, even if they are well-intended in their care. Many others have no natural interest in children because they are simply here to do other things.

In many cases, parents who outwardly show extreme interest in the well-being of their children are attempting to hide their own inner disinterest. This disinterest is often a reflection of how their own parents felt about them. When parents cannot face their own disinterest, they inflict on their children an outward form of extreme interest, which causes these parents to do all the wrong things at all the wrong times.

Parental responses to children also have something to do with the parents' relationship between themselves as husband and wife. The fact that most people are improperly mated has already been discussed. The fact that most parents are improperly mated frequently means they will not be able to stimulate natural parenting skills in each other. Couples generally bring out the worst characteristics in one another, which is why they never become friends. Parents usually stimulate the worst in each other where their children are concerned. Many single parents can tell you that their parenting skills improved after they separated from their spouses. Part of the improvement is simply due to not having someone around who brings out the other's worst behaviors.

On rare occasions, two people come together and activate the best in one another as a couple and/or as parents. Their children demonstrate this fact. These children are usually simple and natural in their approaches to life. They are not often college bound because college for most students is only a way of fulfilling parents' hopes and fantasies, not their own. Ironically, these children are usually not perceived as successful by society's standards and would not be regarded as examples of good, healthy, positive parenting.

Preparation for Parenthood

Most educated parents in Western societies resent their children. They resent them partly because they feel the damages in themselves being activated by the children's presence. However, the main reason for their resentment is that the parents are so ill-prepared to have children and take care of them. It is bad enough that most souls are magnetically attracted by their own damages into the wrong families. It is even worse that these souls cannot ever find what they need to grow within these families. However, it is an even greater tragedy that children can attend school for twelve years and graduate without knowing anything about becoming a parent and raising healthy children.

Education treats boys as though they will never become fathers or have responsibilities as husbands and parents. Education teaches them nothing about what it means to be a man and to fulfill the natural role of teaching their sons and daughters about the physical world. Children learn to relate to the outside world through their fathers. Most high school boys cannot change a fuse or repair a washer in a faucet. How can they possibly help their children to make the proper connections into the physical world?

Girls are expected to learn about family life in home economics. Home economics teachers are often among the most disturbed women in the school system. Many of them are so mentally incompetent that they are incapable of having families of their own. Many of them are single women who can barely function in society, and they are education's idea of preparing young women to become wives and mothers. Women, too, have natural functions within the home. They are the ones who must set the tone for the environment inside the home. They set the stage for how, when, and where the children's needs will be tended.

Most young women graduate from high school without any idea about what parenting means. In fact, education so devalues mothering that most women experience themselves as personal failures when they elect to spend their time mothering. Many finally establish careers outside their homes simply to preserve their own dignity and integrity. In a healthy society, mothering is held in high esteem. Mothers are regarded as the backbone of the society, and much is done to insure that they receive proper comfort and care as mothers.

In Western societies, mothers are trash. House pets get better treatment from family members than most mothers receive. Women fight back by trying to swing into the male polarity with more aggressive behaviors and responses to life. This only further compounds the problem.

Young adults discover very quickly that they know nothing about raising children. Many young couples begin to fear parenthood and failure even during pregnancy. They begin to build up feelings of failure even before their children are born because they know that they are so ill-prepared to have children.

The parents' feelings of failure quickly turn to resentment toward their children. The resentment is directed at the children because the children's very existence causes the parents to feel they have failed. Parents do not see that the educational system failed them. They do not see that there is nothing wrong with them. There is only something very wrong with a system that keeps people locked up for twelve years without teaching them anything about becoming parents and raising healthy children.

Because parents do not know that education has failed them, they blame their children for their own incompetence. This only makes an already impossible situation worse. It means there is no hope for parents and children to untangle things. Sending children to school where they will be abused makes sense if parents already resent their children and feel that their children have caused them pain. In the end, nobody wins but the school system. Parents hurt, children hurt, and schools go on as if education had nothing to do with it.

Childbirth Preparation

Children are most often literally born into the damage of the parents. The fact that children are magnetically pulled to that part of the parent which is damaged and cannot possibly provide proper parenting has already been mentioned. The type of damage in the child always matches the type of damage in the parent. For example, if a parent was damaged in a way that left her vulnerable to people who were abusive and hungry for power, that parent would attract abusive, power-hungry souls as children, over whom she would have no healthy or positive control. If a parent had damages as a result of past neglect, that parent would attract more neglect. That parent might attract needy souls who have been so neglected that they are starving for proper care. But they will not receive it because the mother or father is too bankrupt from their own experiences of neglect to provide what is needed.

This clashing of damages begins during pregnancy and childbirth. Women today are having great difficulty giving birth because their babies are literally pushing their way through the most damaged and vulnerable aspects of the mother's consciousness. Childbirth education has only made matters worse. Childbirth education teaches people to believe that childbirth should be some picture-perfect, peak experience. It teaches women to think there is something wrong with them when they are not elated during labor and delivery. It teaches parents to think that something is wrong with them when they do not feel bonded or connected to their babies. Usually there is just too much damage in the way for anyone to feel bonded.

Childbirth education has caused parents, particularly women, to feel they have failed at something critical to themselves as parents when they are not able to have totally natural, perfect childbirth. These feelings of personal defeat add to the failure parents experience when they discover they know nothing about raising healthy children. These combined failures only lead to more resentment toward the children, because the parents' human egos perceive their children as the ones inciting these feelings. People cannot see that childbirth education has failed them just as their years in schools did. In childbirth education classes, expectant parents are shown pictures and diagrams of babies being born. They are taught to memorize stages of labor and to time their labor contractions, activities which could not be more meaningless. Parents are led to believe that by looking at pictures and memorizing the terms they are prepared for the reality of giving birth to a child. This is the same approach that modern education uses when it teaches children to think they know something about the real world because they saw pictures of Germany, England, and Belgium in a geography book and memorized facts about these countries. The pictures and facts in the geography book have nothing to do with real life and real people in Germany or any other country.

Childbirth education fills parents with false ideas and fantasies about childbirth. It only causes parents more fear, worry, and concern because what they learn in class is so far away from the reality of having a baby. Whenever a person is caught in such a bind between what is being said and what is real, the human consciousness suffers strain. Over a long period of time, it is damaged. Religions cause damage because the ministers are so unlike Jesus, and the discrepancy between who they are as people and what they are saying about Jesus is so great that it causes people strain and eventual damage. Modern education does the same thing to children every day. By the time children graduate from high school they have had to release their own hold on reality just to release the strain.

Childbirth educators are just like school teachers. They are damaged people. They are often the ones who had the worst kinds of childbirth experiences. Except in extremely rare cases, they end up using their roles as educators to pass along their own damages to other parents, by setting up would-be parents for certain failure. Childbirth educators are dangerous people. Many of them incite physicians—who often dislike women—into hurting patients and performing unnecessary medical procedures. They pretend to be rescuers. Just like school teachers who persecute children in the name of good education, they set vulnerable adults up for failure and disappointment.

The more radical the childbirth educator claims to be, the more damaged and dangerous she or he probably is. The more verbal she is about fighting the system, the more she is covertly damaging the parents. There are few and rare exceptions to this, but those who claim to be the exceptions are the most damaged and most destructive. This whole scenario is even further compounded by the fact that the more damaged parents tend to attract the most destructive childbirth educators and the most disturbed physicians—a combination that makes childbearing, particularly in Western societies, a virtual nightmare.

Physicians also tend to enter those fields in which they can best pass along their damages. Pediatrics often attracts men and women who do not like children. Most parents can tell you that they feel very bad after they take their children to the pediatrician. They are not comforted by the fact that their children are often helped, because the parents can actually feel the pediatrician's dislike and mistreatment of the child. The major cause of infant mortality in the United States (which has one of the highest infant mortality rates among developed nations) is that pediatricians, especially, do not like babies, and do not want to treat them medically.

The same situation exists with obstetrics and gynecology. Men and women who do not like women tend to be attracted as physicians to these specialities. Many women perceive this but actually find it comforting because their own distorted ideas about sex tell them they should not go to gynecologists and obstetricians who would like to look at them and touch them. So women are comforted by the coldness and mistreatment they find in the examining room and during labor and delivery.

Childrearing Practices and Ideas

Humanity has lived without natural instinct and spiritual guidance for so long that people have arrived at extremely incorrect and even bizarre conclusions about how to raise children. The educated "experts" have polluted people with mental ideas about what children need. They have set ridiculous standards for how tall a child should be at a certain age, how much the child should weigh, and what the child should be able to do. They have developed standards for when babies should talk and walk, eat solid food, relate to other children, crawl, give up the breast or the bottle, and read, write, and succeed in school.

These standards are a function of educated minds that are stuffed with ideas about children which have nothing to do with real children in real life. Like the educational system, the standards set by the "child development experts" are based on false assumptions that every child learns at the same rate of speed, has the same needs, and the same interests in life. Nothing could be further from the truth. Many child development "experts" believe that children should start school as early as possible. They convince parents that teaching children to read, write, and memorize when they are two or three will produce children of superior intelligence. Nothing could be further from reality.

The human consciousness is a very tender, delicate mechanism. Children under eight or nine years of age are particularly tender. Some children need help with their minds. These are the children with good hearts. Some children need help with their hearts. These are the children with the good minds.

In order for children to learn without being damaged, they must be treated with great tenderness and care. Adults must be very careful of what they present to children and how they present it. People do not know what this means. Most parents have the idea that they should keep their children from finding out about sex. Yet in reality, children are much more damaged from spending their lives in school than they could ever be if they spent their childhoods discovering and experimenting with sex.

Parents do not understand that if their children already have good minds, they do not need to develop their minds. Children with mental gifts do not need to be fed data. They will easily pick up any mental skills they need. A couple of years of reading, writing, and arithmetic at age nine or ten would give them much more than they would need to have satisfying lives.

The television series "Family Ties" is a very popular show. It works because Alex Keaton, played by Michael J. Fox, portrays a know-it-all who keeps discovering that he has a heart. Alex Keaton is a self-promoting bore until he gives something from his heart to others.

If a person has a lot of mind, it is not very likely that he has a lot of heart. Kids with good mental gifts need to be taken around and shown where the problems are and how they can help. Instead, these children are the ones who are taken on some self-centered path through education which allows them no growth at all.

Parents should ask themselves what percentage of great American presidents were really precocious kids? What percentage of great military generals were precocious kids? What percentage of honest building contractors, who build safe homes at fair prices, were precocious kids? What percentage of great writers, architects, and world leaders were precocious kids? What percentage of great teachers (there are some, but they are few) were precocious kids?

People who do great deeds for humanity are always people who are touched by something in life that moves them to do great deeds beyond their capacity. The problem is that when these great events happen, no one in humanity is listening. The best doctors in the world today are the ones who struggled through medical school and were pained by the experience. The honest lawyers are not the ones who graduated in the top five percent of their classes. They are the ones who work for people who need their help for one-tenth the amount of a highly-paid lawyer from a prestigious law firm. So why are parents trying to turn their kids into self-promoting bores like Alex Keaton—and even worse, bores who will never discover their own hearts?

The world is not going to celebrate the people who were great students. The highest awards in the world are given for helping someone else in need. This is true in the military and in the police and fire departments. It is true among politicians, teachers, and citizens in general. Schools are the only places where awards are given to people for helping only themselves. The students who drop out of high school, kick around for awhile, go to trade school, and become builders make a much larger contribution to the world through the simple act of building a house than the average person in Mensa.

Every parent can see that something happens to children when they go to school. Parents can see that children lose their natural softness and tenderness. This softness should be with people throughout their lives. But instead, children get depressed because they discover that the world is not going to serve them and help them grow up.

Children are very, very vulnerable. Their mental vehicles are fragile and require great care. When parents attempt to force linear data into young children, their children get very badly injured. It may appear to the parents and the experts that the children are advancing mentally, but in fact they are not. Trying to force linear data into the mental vehicles is like putting gasoline in your car radiator. The radiator was designed to be filled with water and to be used only in this way. Pouring gasoline into your car radiator would be considered destructive and even insane. Pouring linear data into the mental vehicles of young children is equally destructive and insane. Children's mental vehicles need experiential, nonlinear data in the way that car radiators need water. Anything else ruins the mechanisms that make the child function properly.

When parents attempt to teach children about the world with pictures and words, children begin to experience the world and reality as though it is all flat and lifeless. This experience is very discouraging to them. It flattens them out inside and causes them to feel debilitated by life rather than energized by it.

For instance, if you show children pictures of China with words to describe the pictures, the children conclude that China is the pictures. They conclude that having seen the pictures, they have been to China. They further conclude that China is a flat, boring place. Later on, when someone brings up the subject of China, some children respond with the feeling that they have been there. Because they once saw some pictures of people working in rice paddies, or a photo of the Great Wall, they believe they have seen China.

If the children are shown enough pictures and given enough words they conclude that the world is a flat, boring place. Some children also conclude that having seen the pictures, they have been around the world. If children are shown enough pictures and given enough words about life, they conclude that life is flat, boring, and also meaningless—a conclusion that is very evident in the lifestyles of many educated Westerners.

Children do not belong in classrooms. But if people persist in sending them to school as it now exists, they could at least wait until children are eight or nine, and have passed their most vulnerable years. Even then, current teaching approaches flatten and depress children. If the experts insist on teaching children about China, then at least give children some experience of China. The best way to do this is to take the children to China. If this is not possible, bring two or three Chinese people to the class dressed in their native clothing. Speaking in their native language and through an interpreter, have the Chinese people describe to the children their life in China. Although second hand, the children would then have some small experience of China. Direct experiences enliven and energize the human consciousness. Direct experiences promote evolution. Flat, boring pictures deaden the consciousness and cause children to become involutionary and despairing of life.

Everything in education is turned around backward. Everything in childrearing is also backward, which is why education can continue. There are countless instances in which this is true.

For example, many parents of the 1950s learned from the "experts" that children should be fed at four-hour intervals without exception. They believed and still would say that this feeding schedule produces healthy children. For some souls, these schedules actually cause more damage and pain. This is particularly true for souls who suffered from starvation in past lives and need to be fed when they are hungry in order to begin correcting this damage. This is also true for souls who had lifetimes of experiences that bred internal rigidity. For these souls, rigid feeding schedules only lay the foundation for another lifetime of rigidity, when what is actually needed is a more flexible environment.

For other souls, rigid feeding schedules actually provide comfort and stability in life. These are the souls in need of something stable which they can count on in life, and feeding schedules provide the basis for that stability. We would estimate that about fifty percent of all souls could actually benefit from feeding schedules, while the other fifty percent are only driven further into damage by them. The bigger problem is the fact that everything is so backward that the souls who could benefit from the feeding schedules cannot attract the families who use them.

Since the 1950s, parents have become more and more preoccupied with their children's achievements and status. Since most parents have children because of their own damages and needs, they want their children to look right and succeed at doing the expected things at the correct times, according to the external standards of the experts. Parents have less and less tolerance for children who do not fit within the bell curve of life or within the normal range. For instance, in parents' minds children who walk "early" or talk "early" are products of good parenting in the same way that children who succeed in school are considered products of good parenting. In reality, children who had proper parenting in early childhood—which only a handful of children receive—would be repelled by the school system. The healthiest, most natural students in any school system are often the students who are trying to get out. If schools did not inflict so much failure on school dropouts, they would be the ones to live the most natural lives. In a natural society, children should be ready to "drop out" of school at fourteen or fifteen years of age. They should be ready to launch themselves into adult life, to go out into the world and find out more about what they want to do and where they want to be. They could then, after several years of exploration, return to school to pursue certain subjects relevant to what they wanted to do with their lives.

In a way, this is what dropouts are trying to do. They are trying to get themselves out into the world to find what they want to do and where they want to do it. Society, under the influence of modern education, makes this search impossible by branding dropouts as failures. A few dropouts do discover that there are things they want to do. They are sometimes the ones who return to night school to get more specific education in order to do what they want.

The most "successful" students in any classroom are usually the ones who are products of the worst parenting. They are the ones who are driven to do well by their parents' damages. These children are the ones who are trying to help their parents cover up their own failures and hurts through the success of the children. These are the parents who use their children to avoid looking at their own lives. By using their children's academic successes they can cover up the things they do not want to see in themselves and in their relationships.

We have discussed how parents have collected even more disturbed ideas about their children's achievements in recent years, and how middle class parents of the 1960s decided that lower income children in Head Start Programs were not going to get ahead of their children. They resolved to push their children harder and start them in preschools much earlier.

Parents of the 1980s have taken these disturbed ideas of what is normal and healthy for a child even further. They have concluded that their children should be a certain weight and height at a certain age. When the children weigh more or less than the established standards, the children are put on special diets, and sometimes even medicated, to move their natural body weights within the "norms." Some children who are not tall enough to meet the established normal height requirements are given drugs to induce their growth. Anything that is not "normal," perfect, and within the assigned standards of the "experts" is open to condemnation and alteration.

This approach to childrearing is a function of the same disturbed value system that causes Western society to focus on glamour and physical perfection rather than spiritual perfection. It is the same value system Hitler used to justify murdering millions of Jews in Germany when he tried to perfect the Aryan race. It produces very unbalanced, disturbed children who cannot break away from the damage that is done because everything natural about them has been condemned and changed.

It should be noted here that parents tend to get their standards of measurement from psychologists and physicians who claim to be offering advice and aid. For instance, when children go for regular physical exams, physicians tell parents whether the children are of "normal" height and weight. The school psychologists administer school intelligence tests and then tell parents whether the children are of average or better intelligence, or whether they are below average and substandard. Who decided how tall or short, fat or thin people should be? Who decided that children should be measured for intelligence (as if I.Q. tests measured something other than memory)? The answer is that people decided—some of the most disturbed and destructive people in society, who do not like children and want them to hurt because they themselves hurt and cannot find relief.

Passing the Damage

Parents pass their damages along to children in many ways. The false standards and incorrect ideas about measuring children are only part of a very grim picture. Most damages are passed on from one generation to another without any consciousness or awareness of doing this. If most parents were fully conscious of how they were damaging their children, they would be overwhelmed with pain because most parents are well-intended people who do not set out to destroy their children.

The process of passing damage from parent to child is very subtle. It is done over a period of years and with continuous reinforcement.

Each child usually absorbs some aspect of the parents' damages depending on the individual child's vulnerabilities. As an example, a parent may have three children. The first child might be vulnerable to the parent's feelings of personal failure and may become a failure in order to act out the parent's damage in this area. The second child of the same parent may be vulnerable to that parent's angry feelings toward the opposite sex. This child may act out the parent's anger by becoming gay or attracting a long list of disturbed marriage relationships which serve to prove the parent's point. The third child in the family may be vulnerable to the parent's mental worries and fears. That child may develop a phobia of heights or dogs or anything else as a way of acting out the parent's damage.

Most parents can remember promising themselves they would never become like their own parents. Yet if they look at their lives, they will see that they now do with their own children the very things they promised never to do. They do these things because the human consciousness automatically absorbs anything it does not like or strongly resists. The things that people dislike most about their parents are the areas of damage they are most vulnerable to absorbing.

There are many formulas for passing damage along. Again, these acts are usually done unconsciously as a way for a person to cope with the world. Having damage is like having a broken leg. People adjust to it and get around with it, and soon they forget that their leg is broken. They forget they have developed so many ways of coping and adjusting.

These formulas are as unique and varied as there are souls, although some have a common thread. For instance, to render a child incompetent you must first discover with which parent the child has identified, and then block the child from having any contact with that parent when the parent is acting in a competent way. In a short time, the child begins to experience himself or herself as incompetent.

Parents give children many different messages about how they want them to be in school. The children who usually do well in school are the ones whose parents want them to do well. Conversely, many of the children who do poorly in school do so because that is what their parents want them to do. Some parents want their children to do well sometimes, and to be unsuccessful other times. These children become sporadic achievers in school.

Parents convey these expectations covertly and without words. They are often a function of the parents' damages, or of some behavioral system they constructed to protect damages. Schools never account for these very powerful messages which parents inadvertently convey to children every day. The more the parental expectation is inconsistent with the child's natural interests and abilities, the more damaged that child will become.

For example, if you are a parent who did well in school because you had a very good memory, you may secretly not want your child to do better than you. Maybe your child also has specific memory abilities and the interest to do very well in school. You may perceive your own child as a threat to your system and discourage that child from doing his or her best. If the gap is wide enough between what you as a parent want the child to do and what the child is able and interested in doing, that child will develop problems. It is further likely that none of these problems will out-manifest in a way that would lead you to discover the source of your child's difficulty.

Another common situation is the parent who wants the child to succeed in school to compensate for his or her own personal failures. This again becomes particularly damaging if the child does not have the memory ability or natural interests which would allow him to respond to the parent's expectations. The result is that again the child will develop problems—none of which will manifest in such a way that would lead the parent to their source.

Then, there are parents who want their children to do well to compensate for the parents' failures, but also resent the children's success because it makes the parents more aware of their own failures. These children live in a gap created by the conflicting messages they receive every day. They are the children who do well one week and poorly the next.

Teachers often perceive these children as deliberately trying to avoid doing their schoolwork or as having periods of laziness. Most teachers respond to sporadic learners with anger and punishment because teachers cannot count on these students to make them look good. The results for these children could not be worse. Most of them conclude that they will never win at anything they do in life. Most suffer an endless low level depression and despair which only becomes worse when teachers punish them for their inconsistencies.

The point is that every child sitting in a classroom today is trying to cope with all kinds of overt and covert messages from parents and teachers. Neither parents nor teachers ever account for this reality when they are responding to children's successes and failures. By the time children grow up, these adapted behaviors are institutionalized in their consciousnesses in a way that makes them forget how it was for them as children. This renders them incapable of responding to the real burdens they must face during their childhoods and in their adult lives.

10

EDUCATION & SPIRITUAL DESTRUCTION

NOTE: This is a book about reality. Reality is not positive. Reality is extremely negative.

PEOPLE COME TO this planet in order to grow spiritually. There is no other reason for human existence, regardless of any religious fantasies about life and death that people have invented. Most people think of themselves in terms of their names, their families, friends, where they live, their careers, their beliefs, and their feelings. Yet these only describe aspects of the human personality and its current personal preferences.

When people die they usually do not remember where they lived, with whom they lived, or what they did for a living. Many people do not remember their names or what they were doing when they died. All of this simply disappears at death as these are all aspects of the human world. It is hard for people to understand how this could be true because they have lived by their religious fantasies for so long, and have invested so much of themselves into human goals and accomplishments.

In the human world, every parent has certain goals and expectations for each of their children. In their early years, children automatically attempt to respond to the goals and expectations of their parents, even though those goals and expectations are rarely in the best interests of the children. As the children grow older, they discover that attempting to live by their parents' goals is not correct for them. The children naturally rebel and attempt to live in some other way. However, over time, they build up feelings of guilt which propel them right back into living by their parents' goals.

Every human being is subject to these polarities. Everyone swings between trying to live according to their parents' goals and expectations, rebelling against them, and then swinging right back into trying to live by them. This is the nature of the human world. The only way a person can break free from this cycle is through spiritual intervention.

Each human ego structure is an extension of its own original spiritual creator called the Monad. The Monad is the spiritual part of the person and has all the natural rights to the use of the human ego. Each Monad is like a scientist who has invented a robot (the human ego structure) to carry out the prime function of the Monad. The prime function of the Monad is to direct each human ego structure through a series of experiences, over a number of lifetimes, which will allow the Monad to fulfill his or her own spiritual requirements.

In the age of darkness, the human ego structures—the robots—were easily damaged and broken. They set off on their own, ignoring the directives of the scientists or Monads. Once they broke from their own creators, they were doomed to swing between obedience and rebellion, never to live in a way that was natural and correct.

Over the last one hundred years, modern education and religion have caused that human suffering to double in intensity. Both religion and modern education were designed from the human world to prey upon the vulnerabilities in people that result from damage. Religion preys upon human hurt by telling people they are bad. People hear through religion that there is something evil about them because they cannot stop hurting. They go to churches because they are in pain. They need help. Instead, they get lectures and sermons about how they should lead better lives. The ministers and priests who say these things are not living better lives. The televangelists with their diamond rings, expensive cars, and fancy suits are not living as Jesus lived. The priests who vow to celibacy and then have sex with married women in the parish are not living as Jesus lived. The destruction caused by modern religions is the topic of another book, *Modern Religion and the Destruction of Spiritual Capacity*, which can be read for a more in-depth explanation.

Modern education works the same way as religion. It preys upon the vulnerabilities in children by punishing them and embarrassing them for acting like natural children. It frightens them and threatens them with personal failure each day. It conspires with parents to alienate and isolate children from the real world where their incorrect ideas and feelings resulting from damage could be unraveled. Most children enter the first grade damaged. They graduate destroyed.

Religion and modern education work together. Education disconnects people from reality and religion connects them into fantasy. Together they combine to form a complete denial of all spiritual reality. A true spiritual path is one in which ideas are properly applied to reality. It is one in which a person who flatters himself with false pride one day, knows that he will pay for it with an emotional low or discouragement the next. He knows this as surely as he knows that if he throws a rock into the air, the rock will eventually fall to the ground.

Education and religion promote the same illogical thought processes. These illogical thought processes have led people to believe they can go to church and consume the Logos of this planet as if He were a piece of meat, and then to assume that this will cause them to grow spiritually. People have the audacity to think that they can "eat his body" and "drink his blood" and be saved. This not only refers to the Catholics. All religions have their version of consumption. The Jews believe they can confer with the Logos by standing in front of a wall, barking out prayers and making peculiar gestures. They believe they can call upon the Logos to answer their personal purposes no matter how corrupt those purposes may be.

In a time of light, these ideas will eventually diminish. However, in darkness and in the present transition period from the Age of Darkness, this illogical thinking thrives. These ideas make a mockery of the Logos. They negate all spiritual reality. The Logos was responsible for the creation of this planet. No one is required to consume Him in order to grow spiritually.

All root races who have come to this planet have gone through these absurd thought processes. This present root race, as well as another prior race, have some anomalies within their soul bodies. These anomalies are actually only mildly outside the range of normal. However, when these anomalies are combined with the destructive and illogical thinking processes caused by religion and modern education, the result is a race of self-destructive people who are filled with self-destructive ideas which lead them to the brink of nuclear disaster.

Modern education combined with religion is the straw that has broken humanity's back. It has pushed the human race into more hurt and suffering than people can tolerate without numbing out. Fifty years ago it was still possible for the few relatively undamaged souls to incarnate and grow up listening to the voices of their own Monads. They could live their lives according to some spiritual direction and purpose. Today that is no longer possible. Education has become so completely destructive that *all* children are damaged by the system, especially the "better" students. Even the souls who are less damaged cannot escape destruction after they attend school for two or three years.

The net result is that spiritual growth on this planet has all but ceased. Religion and education are credited with the final blows which have so destroyed humanity that people cannot move forward spiritually. Everyone must now spend hundreds of years just healing the hurt and correcting the misinformation that prevents them from doing the only things they came here to do.

Every soul on this planet not only has a unique mission or purpose but must also complete the seven planetary initiations in the process of fulfilling that purpose. The seven initiations are steps or stages in a person's spiritual growth. Each person must fulfill the requirements of each step before that level of vibration can be achieved. Volume One in this series contains more information about these steps. We cannot give people any detailed information about how to accomplish these initiations. Humanity has so much healing to do that such information would only go into the damaged, disturbed, mental vehicles of people, and could not be accurately received. Even if the information could be received, people would not have the resources to follow Our directions. Education and religion have bankrupted people. They cannot grow until they rebuild these resources, which for most people will take a very long time.

As it is, there are people who have read Volume One and have already started to misuse the limited information that We did provide. Many of the New Age spiritual types have concluded that they have already accomplished levels of evolution which they will not actually reach for thousands of years, even if they were able to start today. Others have concluded that they are now following the advice of their own spiritual directives, when in fact they are listening to the echoes of their own minds. Still others believe they need only study boatbuilding or master some trade or craft in order to evolve.

Even if all the people on this planet could be healed of damage right now, evolution would not automatically resume. Memorizing has destroyed human mental vehicles in ways that will take many lifetimes to unravel and correct. Religion and education have filled people with misinformation which must be corrected before most souls can begin moving forward again.

To accomplish spiritual growth, a soul must be able to hear and follow the directives of its own Monad. It must follow these directives in the proper order, and fulfill them at exactly the right time. This means that people need to be surrounded by an environment which allows them to accomplish what they are being told to do. So they must not only be healed of past damages that might prevent them from hearing directives, but they also need to attract circumstances where they can carry out those directives.

Schools do not provide environments in which souls can grow. If anyone was actually growing spiritually, they would have to fail in the current school system to achieve spiritual success. In order for souls to grow, people must be willing to sacrifice temporary human goals for spiritual goals. Schools only direct students to achieve human goals.

The people who "succeed" in schools are often the younger souls who have not accumulated enough experiences to see how destructive and toxic education has become. They are vulnerable to the approval of teachers and school officials, and are too frightened not to please them. They are also vulnerable to academic competition. Successful students fall for the idea that competing for information is stimulating, motivating, and a good way to learn, when in reality it is deadly.

There is a way in which competition can be very healthy, but not the way that school systems ask children to compete. In school there are winners and losers. Students only succeed because others have failed. If all the students in a class do well, educators conclude that the teacher is being too lenient.

In the spiritual world there are only winners. People compete for quality, not for information. They compete for improvement and for higher qualities and standards of excellence, not for useless information and speed. Imagine, for instance, five people who want to build boats. One person may build a beautiful, crafted sailboat. The other four look at that sailboat, admire it, and use it to inspire themselves to build something even better. Then five more boat-builders come along. They look at all five boats and see the quality in those boats. They admire them and use them to inspire themselves to build something better. Everyone is competing to achieve a higher quality of excellence and perfection. Everyone needs everyone else to succeed, otherwise there is nothing toward which anyone can aim. Within this kind of competition, each time a new boat is built the standards of quality are raised.

In schools, people only succeed at the expense of someone else. There is nothing to improve because the subject matter is worthless in the first place. Students succeed by learning to show disrespect and disregard for the work of others. Anyone else's failure is perceived as a chance for someone else to get ahead.

Any evolving soul could not function in this system. If Jesus were alive today, he would be a high school dropout. He would probably become an auto mechanic or a carpenter and live a very simple life. Formal education would only have stood in his way.

Many older souls refuse to compete for useless information. They can see that education will not take them anywhere, so they simply will not use their resources to destroy themselves. These students are commonly seen as discipline problems. They have more accumulations and experiences, and are usually not so vulnerable to the teachers' approval or disapproval. These souls are more able to see teachers for what they are. Teachers ignore them as much as possible because they do not want these older souls to expose them for what they are.

Educators believe that education alters a person's destiny. They think that when they categorize children into so-called "tracking" systems, they as educators can then shape and form another person's destiny. Individual destiny is predetermined by the individual soul. Children are in school because of their individual destinies. Educators do not bring any child to a new destiny.

Education actually limits children's opportunities to manifest their individual destinies. It causes children to think in terms of very limited social roles. Children are taught to see themselves as potential lawyers, doctors, teachers, secretaries, nurses, or engineers. They are discouraged from imagining themselves as great artists, musicians, inventors, carpenters, plumbers, welders, and electricians. They are not taught to see themselves as individual human beings with specific needs, wants, interests, talents, and instincts. And they are certainly never told to think of themselves as individual souls with specific spiritual destinies and specific tasks to accomplish.

Education is like a game of "Hollywood Squares" where each student is placed in a specific, limited box and then rarely allowed outside of that box. Educators pretend that by "tracking" students or placing them in boxes, they can alter personal destiny. There is no evidence in reality to support this conclusion. In fact, all evidence suggests that just the opposite is true. Destiny is always a function of the spiritual world and has nothing to do with one's experiences in the classroom.

Calamity and Growth

Souls must be able to collect direct life experiences to acquire the spiritual accumulations necessary for evolution to occur. They must be able to go out into the world and continuously experience life directly. Through direct experiences, souls establish a body of knowledge, or accumulations, which allows them to detach themselves more and more from the physical world.

In a sense, souls grow through calamity. Most people do not realize it, but they are actually living within a schedule of events. People only become aware of the schedule when they collide with an event. When you burn your finger on a hot stove, you collide with an event. When your wife leaves you for another man, you collide with an event. When your oil burner breaks down in mid-January, you collide with an event. These events are experienced as calamities. Some are minor calamities while others are, or seem to be, much more serious.

Each time a person collides with an event, that person has an opportunity to discover something about reality. He or she has an opportunity to make a connection between cause and effect. Most calamities teach people about the temporary nature of the human world and the futility of investing in human goals. When people collect enough calamities, they gradually stop pursuing human goals and start pursuing spiritual goals. However, this can only occur after the person collects enough direct experiences to be absolutely certain that human goals will not bring peace and satisfaction, and that spiritual goals are, in the long run, more valuable and fulfilling.

For most souls, discovering human reality takes a long, long time, even under the best of circumstances. Modern education has completely disrupted this process by confining souls to classrooms and preventing children from collecting direct experiences of reality. Modern education has established an extremely rigid classroom life, governed completely by the human goals and interests of educators and school officials. After schools disconnect souls from the physical world they then fill children with incorrect mental ideas which prevent them from establishing cause and effect. Once souls are disconnected from cause and effect, all evolution ceases. It ceases because people are no longer able to learn from even the most painful calamities.

For instance, Bill decides to fulfill his human goals for continuous excitement by engaging in a long string of meaningless sexual relationships. Throughout his activities, he feels alienated, lonely, and more and more angry at the women he is sleeping with. Some of these sexual encounters are very exciting, but the excitement is temporary. Therefore, his desire for excitement must continuously increase in order to avoid the alienation these relationships are causing him. Over the years, Bill has many sexual encounters. He still feels bad, but never stops his encounters.

When people have been able to establish the proper connections between cause and effect in the physical world, they can then use these same mechanisms to understand many areas of life, including human relationships. When these connections are destroyed, people cannot make the proper connections in any areas of life. If Bill had been able to establish the right systems for determining cause and effect, he may have been able to stop his meaningless sex life after two or three encounters. Thanks to modern education, his mechanisms for establishing cause and effect have been destroyed. His life is a series of calamities, but he cannot connect the fact that his desire for excitement is the source of his problem. Instead of learning from his distressed feelings, he increases the very activity that is making him feel so bad. This is exactly what educated people do after cause and effect is destroyed and they are forced to live from their minds.

The more education destroys cause and effect in people the more incapable and unconscious they become. People become incapable of making good decisions. The American Congress is a perfect example. The Senate and House of Representatives are supposed to be composed of America's finest leaders. Yet, as a group these people can barely manage to pass legislation correcting an unfair tax system, which everyone agrees is unfair. These are the people who authorize the construction of navy aircraft carriers with billion-dollar price tags which can be put out of commission with one small missile. Leaders of state governments vote to raise the speed limit to sixty-five miles per hour, knowing that it will probably cause an increase in highway fatalities.

The more incapable people become, the more unconscious and asleep they are. The story of modern education is the story of a woman who arrives home from grocery shopping and finds her husband in bed with another woman. Her husband looks at her and says, "This is just a dream. If you go outside and come back through that door in five minutes, you will see that this is not real."

So she goes outside and he gets up. The other woman sneaks out the back door. He quickly makes the bed, and goes into the living room. His wife re-enters through the front door with the groceries. He says, "Hi honey, it's good to see you." She says, "Hi, it's good to see you as well."

Bill, and millions of other souls like him, will waste their lives. They will not only be unable to accomplish evolution but will actually cause themselves more damage. What is even worse is that they cannot re-establish cause and effect at death since this can only be accomplished in the physical world. They must come back into the physical world and attempt to do it again. Each time they come back in, they are more damaged than they were in their previous lifetime. They are also likely to continue attracting school systems which undo the connections they might make in early childhood. These souls must repeat the same going-nowhere patterns for hundreds and even thousands of years, until cause and effect can be reinstated.

Vigilance

If everything on earth was functioning properly, souls would be learning about new aspects of reality every day. Each lifetime would provide people with exactly the right opportunities to make exactly the right connections with reality. Over a period of life-times, each soul would naturally accumulate enough experiences to accomplish the seven planetary initiations. There would be no long periods of interruption of the evolutionary process, or any wasted lifetimes where no understanding or experience was gained.

People would also readily develop something called vigilance. Vigilance is watchfulness or awareness of reality. It is referred to in the *I Ching* as resoluteness, and it develops as people resolve that the human world is full of calamities which cannot be avoided. Vigilance develops when people begin to see that unless they keep a close and watchful eye on the human ego, the ego will always take off and fulfill its own meaningless, temporary goals and desires.

Vigilance grows as people accumulate enough experiences to teach them how the world works. For instance, some people like the idea of "falling in love." They have not yet learned enough about reality to know that people who "fall in love" always "fall out of love." People who say they have fallen in love really mean they have found someone who matches their mental pictures of a perfect mate. It means that sooner or later they will become dis-appointed and dissatisfied with the "beloved." When they become dissatisfied and disappointed enough, they will throw the "be-loved" out of their lives. They will then start searching again until they find someone else with whom they can "fall in love."

The vigilant person knows ahead of time that falling in love is deadly. He or she may still go out and do it, but with enough consciousness to know where it is going. If he can really catch on, he can use his disappointment to grow, and to possibly become real friends with the once beloved partner—if he is very vigilant, and very lucky.

Modern education forces children away from reality in a way that prevents them from gaining vigilance. In fact, schools are run on unconsciousness and unawareness which are the exact opposite of vigilance. Vigilance is absolutely necessary for souls to acquire. They must become vigilant or they cannot grow. The more edu-cated people become, the further into unconsciousness they are driven. The more unconscious they become, the more painful their lives are.

Vigilance does not prevent a person from colliding with reality. Everyone is always subject to collision with the events in their schedule. The transiting moon alone, moving through the astrological chart, sets off one series of events every month. There are many other influences which produce an individual schedule of events that even the most vigilant consciousness cannot avoid. However, the vigilant person is driving along the highway of life at twenty or thirty miles an hour, because he or she knows that sooner or later there will be potholes in the road and barriers to avoid. The vigilant person is navigating through life, not just cruising blindly down the road.

The non-vigilant person is cruising at ninety miles per hour with a blindfold covering his eyes. He is certain that he is on the road to success and personal improvement. He sees himself as being free to do anything with his life, with whomever he chooses, and feels that he will never have difficulties. Then suddenly, he discovers a pothole in the road or runs into a wall that he did not see. He crashes much harder and faster than the vigilant person. If he is lucky and learns quickly, he figures out something about life. If not, he just gets back out on the road and starts cruising into unconsciousness once again. Some people crash so hard and fast that it takes them lifetimes to get back up on their feet.

Education teaches children nothing about the highway of life. No one tells children that sometimes you really have to bite the bullet. No one explains that there will be times in a child's life when someone she likes or loves will not want to have anything to do with her—or vice versa. No one says that at sometime in their lives they will lie to someone and wish afterward that they had not. No one tells them that some people can have very fulfilling lives as sharecroppers while other people would find sharecropping a nightmare. No one tells the children that some people have very empty lives and die impoverished, even though they were financially quite wealthy. No one advises them that life can only be measured in terms of satisfaction, not human success.

No one ever tells those children who appear to be coasting through life that they are not learning anything. No one points out the fact that those children have no ability to understand people. No one ever informs children that the most "successful" students in their classes have not a trace of compassion for the problems of others.

Education does not teach children that good people lose their steady boyfriends and girlfriends. Education does not teach children that lying is a normal thing to do and that most people feel bad when they do it. Education will not acknowledge that failure hurts. Instead, schools use normal life experiences to make people feel bad about themselves. This causes students to numb out on life so that every normal event becomes a painful calamity, simply because they are so unconscious and so unprepared.

Duration and Time

In the human world, where people are focused on human goals, life is structured in units of time. Most people live according to very rigid schedules and are, for the most part, completely ruled by time. Time in the human world is a function of death. When people organize their lives and measure their accomplishments around time, they are actually organizing their lives in terms of death. All time units have been constructed from the fact that people die.

When people focus on time, and therefore on death, they focus their resources only on what can be accomplished in the human world. In the human consciousness, death signifies the end. When people organize their lives around the end, they try to fulfill all their human desires and objectives before they die. They get the idea that they "only live once" and therefore must fulfill all their dreams before death, even though none of their dreams lead to anything permanent or satisfying. This failure to find satisfaction causes people to feel that their lives will prove to be hopeless and their accomplishments will be meaningless, no matter what they do. In the human sense, this is true.

Schools keep children completely focused on time. Education is probably the most time-oriented system in society. Children are ruled by school years, semesters, quarters, and scheduled classes. Their lives are chopped up into chapters, lesson plans, units, and sections. Schools preoccupy children with time and fill them with human ideas of success and accomplishment, which prevent them from focusing on spiritual objectives.

Schools also use time schedules to avoid change. Schedules keep everything the same. Schedules make people's lives comfortable because they help insulate them from anything that would challenge or confront their ideas about life.

Souls do not function in time units. The spiritual world functions in terms of duration. Duration has to do with change which occurs over time. Souls are not preoccupied with death because souls do not die. When everything is going according to the natural Plan, souls are only focused on evolution and change over time.

Evolutionary changes do not occur in a semester or a school year. Under ordinary circumstances, evolution takes thousands of years and many, many lifetimes. Souls often work at perfecting the same skill for many lifetimes in succession before they have acquired the mastery necessary for evolution to occur. For instance, a great violinist of today probably began playing the violin, or another musical instrument, hundreds of years ago. He may have spent three or four lifetimes developing technical skills alone. He may then have spent another two or three lifetimes learning to play with heart and feeling. Then, finally, all the aspects of learning come together and a master musician is born.

As a young child, this master musician may demonstrate incredible competence and natural talent. However, the competence is a function of seven or eight lifetimes of training coming together in this lifetime. The perfection that people hear in his music is a function of evolutionary change and learning accumulated over hundreds of years.

The same thing is true for most great artists and accomplished craftsmen. Many of them can tell you that they just seemed to know how to paint or build a boat. Many of them have the feeling that they have done this before, but cannot remember where or when.

When people are fulfilling spiritual goals, time passes almost unnoticed. Schools focus children on human goals and on time. Most people can remember watching the clock for hours on end during some school days.

One way to begin to understand duration is to think of a time when you were so involved in something that you lost track of time. Maybe you were working in your garden or hiking in the woods. Perhaps you were building a cabinet or refinishing an old desk, or reading a book that captured your imagination. Remember how surprised you were to find out how much time had passed while you were enjoying yourself? (This is not a perfect example, but it will help you get a sense of duration.)

The requirements of spiritual evolution are unique to each person, but they are almost always the things the person likes to do the most and naturally does well. There are also sacrifices that must be made which are not as easily accomplished, but even the sacrifices lead to more natural, simple ways of life.

People are afraid that if they lived in duration their lives would become chaotic. In reality, it is focusing on time and death which leads people to live chaotic lives. In school, children cannot eat when they are hungry. They cannot go to the bathroom when they need to use it. They cannot talk when they have something to say. They cannot laugh out loud when they think something is funny. They cannot go out and get fresh air when they want to go. They cannot leave the group to be by themselves when they should. They cannot work longer than the scheduled class time on projects which interest them. They cannot do anything unless it is time to do it. And the school decides when it is time.

This kind of rigid scheduling is what causes chaos and confusion in children's lives. By the time students graduate from high school, they do not know when they are hungry, tired, in need of privacy, restless, or in need of conversation. They only know how to schedule their lives, and how to live by those schedules.

Duration has to do with everything that is natural. It has to do with change that occurs naturally and not because the bell rang. It has to do with instinctually knowing when it is "time to sow and time to reap" so that change can occur with maximum efficiency. Duration has to do with the evolutionary journey each soul must take, and with all the natural evolutionary changes that occur along the way.

Perfection

Spiritual evolution is not only a process of accumulating information about reality, and of establishing a mechanism that allows for the proper connections between cause and effect. It is also a process of accomplishing spiritual perfection. This spiritual perfection must be expressed out in some way in the physical world if the person is living in a physical body. Each level of initiation requires a higher and higher degree of perfection. Each level requires a more refined expression of that perfection.

Spiritual perfection is nothing like the human ideas of perfection. In fact, when people are not accomplishing spiritual perfection they attempt to find perfection in the human world. Hitler's idea of human perfection has already been discussed. Hitler wanted to develop a perfect physical race and decided to purge the planet of anyone who did not fit his ideas of physical perfection. Hitler and Stalin represent some of the worst outbreaks of darkness in human history. They also demonstrate what can happen when people lose focus on perfecting themselves spiritually.

The educational system seeks human perfection. Educators have decided that only the children with good memories will survive within the school setting. All others will be condemned to personal failure and worthless lives. The educational system has decided that only people who attend college have the right to a good life. Everyone else is to be devalued and treated with disrespect.

As previously mentioned, many parents, influenced by modern education, have decided that only tall, thin children are acceptable. Heavy-set children must diet and short children must take hormones, so that all children can be physically perfect.

These ideas are true signs of the aftermath of darkness. The idea of perfection is correct, but the manifestations in the human world could not be more distorted. Evolution is a process of purifying and perfecting the consciousness. It has nothing to do with how much people can remember or what they look like in physical appearance.

In order to express spiritual perfection (and to learn more about cause and effect) souls must be able to acquire skills. They might, for example, need to make things in wood, turn a bowl on a lathe, use a potter's wheel, or learn how to take pictures and develop them. Each soul requires different skills to express its own unique level and variety of perfection. Some souls need skills in electricity. Others need to know about plumbing. Some need to become welders, and others sculptors and painters. Souls require skills both to develop some mastery over the physical world and to express that perfection.

Schools would be ideal places for souls to acquire skills. However, the educational system avoids teaching children any skills which would allow them to express excellence and perfection. Children in Russia are far more likely to receive the support they need to develop skills and natural talents—if only to be used by the State as examples of Russian children and their abilities.

To acquire skills, people need competent teachers. They must be taught by skilled men and women who have enough control over their own personal ideas, desires, and impulses to find real joy in their students' successes. They need to be the kinds of teachers who can go into the darkroom and feel joy and satisfaction helping the students develop their negatives. This joy is not the kind of feeling that you would find in a proud parent. It is just the opposite. Proud parents use their children to feel better about themselves.

Education prohibits competence. Schools systematically eliminate competent people to insure institutionalized mediocrity. Students are left without skilled teachers who could teach them the things they need and want to know. Education breeds mediocrity. No one ever becomes skilled at anything by attending school. Parents, caregivers, electricians, plumbers, carpenters, artists, craftspeople, all learn their skills outside the educational system. While in school, no one is ever allowed to learn anything that would benefit them spiritually.

The Road to Evolution

Educators believe that evolution is a process of the physical world rather than the spiritual world. They think that man evolved up from the ape and so on down the line. Evolution is a spiritual world process. Man was always man. Apes did not evolve into men. Souls, however, do work their way up through the plant and animal kingdoms, accumulating matter along the way. This will be the subject of another book many years from now.

Educators do not teach students anything about spiritual evolution because they know nothing about it. If they did, they would not spend their lives in the public educational system. Educators do know how to disconnect students from reality. They promote a kind of anti-evolution by preventing children from finding out what is happening in the world.

Evolution can best be described as the climbing of a mountain. There are only four roads that lead a person up and over or around the mountain. One path is the path of the Sufis. It is a long, tedious road which requires tremendous effort even to travel a short distance. However, if people stick with this path for a very long time, positive results can be achieved.

A second path is the way of the Buddhist. This path goes straight up the side of the mountain to the top. It is a very difficult climb that, again, can only be accomplished very slowly and very carefully. It requires a cloistered life—the Buddhist method for building inner peace. Most souls who follow this way take many lifetimes to go a short distance, but with persistence they too arrive at their destination.

At this time, there are no Buddhist monasteries located in Western society which could foster anyone's evolution. Nor are any Sufi groups in the Western world capable of taking people the full distance. Westerners have borrowed ideas from the Buddhists and Sufis and have tried to Westernize these systems. For instance, they have tried to take the focus and concentration of the Buddhists and adapt that into their own way of life. Americans might decide that if they could meditate for fifteen minutes each day, or some other set amount of time, they would evolve like a Buddhist. At that rate, it would take millions of years to produce any kind of evolution, even if it worked—which it would not. This amount of meditation and focus on a daily basis is so completely outweighed by chaos and pointless living that people would be unable to build the resources necessary to move forward spiritually.

There is a third path which is also common to Eastern spiritual practices. This path might be thought of as the way of the Sages. Seen in this way, Sages are spiritual Regents who have been sent here to act as guideposts for people who are seeking evolution. The Sages are not religious in their nature although they sometimes come into certain religions, such as Hinduism and other religions found in Eastern cultures. There are very few souls, even within Eastern societies, who are able to recognize these Regents or Sages, or to discriminate them from the false gods. Most Easterners are duped by their religions in the way that Westerners are duped by Christianity and Judaism.

Those who follow the way of the Sages are often souls with many occult skills which they have developed over a long period of time. These souls often come into the same situation lifetime after lifetime. They use their occult skills to align themselves with the Sages or spiritual leaders. They must always sort out the old, dead religions from the real spiritual paths. There are no spiritual Regents or Sages currently located within any Western religion or New Age practice.

The fourth path would best be described as the way of the Brotherhood. The Brotherhood is involved in all of the paths that have been mentioned. However, We speak specifically of the fourth path as the way of the Brotherhood because it is necessary for Westerners to comprehend the fact that the Brotherhood is currently only involved in one path for people in Western societies. This is not to say that the Brotherhood is not working with many individuals in the Western world. It is merely to point out the fact that the Brotherhood has only one ashram in the Western world and this ashram is called Gentle Wind. Gentle Wind is a healing project that works primarily to restore the mental-emotional vehicles of people in Western societies. This book and the others in this series are a part of this project. Information about this work can be obtained by writing or calling Gentle Wind at the address or telephone number listed at the end of this book.

Many "eclectic" thinkers find this idea extremely distasteful because in the made-up fantasy world they have developed they believe there are hundreds of roads that will take them over the mountain. They believe there are many New Age techniques, technologies, psychotherapies, and gurus. Those people who want to be eclectic believe they have the right to travel any and all of these paths, in some cases simultaneously. They are correct in thinking that they have the right to do anything they want. What they do not want to see is that none of their paths are leading them anywhere. They take a path because it sounds exciting or promising. Then they discover that the path they have chosen will not take them to the top of the mountain. They climb back down and try another path. Then they discover that the second path will not take them to the top of the mountain either. They climb back down and try another path.

In their attempts to try all the different paths, these eclectics attend weekend workshops, meditation classes, and psychic readings. They seek gurus and channellers who claim to be the real thing. In the process of trying, they use up all their resources. Even if they later discover one of the four roads that will actually take them to the top of the mountain, it is too late. They are too bankrupt to be able to make the climb.

People who believe in the idea of many paths are often the souls who have been destroyed by education. They are competitive academically but they are not spiritually ambitious. They are the people who like to go to New Age "expos" and fairs where they can be entertained in the name of spiritual growth, and where they can talk about their ideas with other people who lack spiritual ambition.

Conclusion

This book was written only to expose the modern educational system for what it is. It was written to challenge the human ideas and values that allow this system to continue, and to lay the foundation for a time when humanity is healed enough to demand something much better.

The educational system as it now exists is an outgrowth of thousands of years of damage and injury to the human consciousness. It has become a powerful and institutionalized machine. It is a system that has a life of its own, one that even educators and school officials cannot control. The best way to describe modern education is to think of it as an eighteen-wheel truck filled with toxic waste. It is careening down the highway and there is no one at the wheel. As the truck flies by, people are expected to celebrate it and praise it as one of humanity's greatest achievements.

Modern education is the second-largest threat to human existence today, standing second only to a nuclear holocaust. It is not yet known whether humanity can bring the nuclear madness under enough control to avoid annihilation. Presently, a nuclear holocaust would be the perfect ending to a four-act play called *The Industrial Revolution*. In this play, all of the characters who have raped the industrial world for personal gain and greed can unite forces with the entire cast of educated scientists who still want to see their nuclear inventions outmanifested.

World leaders everywhere are threatened by the possibility of nuclear destruction. As the leaders of the United States and the Soviet Union scramble to sign arms limitation agreements, people are actually seeking to stop global destruction. At this point in their search, those who would hold off destruction have not even found the pilot light and gas sources that keep the energy of nuclear annihilation alive.

Yet the ideas that govern religious orthodoxy and modern education are the very sources of the flame that Americans and Soviets now seek to extinguish. People could think of the ideas that hold religions together as a mixture of both combustible and poisonous gases. All of these gases are looking for a flame in order to ignite.

The current educational system with all of its pompous ideas is the flame of the pilot light. The human greed of all those who have raped the stock market and destroyed world industry is the oxygen for the flame. The educated scientists looking for the "big bang" are drunk with the idea of a nuclear disaster.

So, assuming humanity can find the pilot light that keeps nuclear destruction alive, and then turn off its combustible source, the next greatest single threat to human survival is modern education. We must be clear that We are not giving this book to humanity so that people will go out and attempt to change this system. People are far too damaged to be able to alter an institutional machine like education. The system is too integrated into society and into people's lives to change through challenge and confrontation. In fact, any attempts to change this system from the human world would only make it more negative and more powerful. We have already discussed what happens when people try to change things from the human world. When famous musicians get together to sing for the benefit of the homeless, homelessness becomes glamorized and increases. When childbirth educators mount campaigns to halt unnecessary Cesarean births, the surgical deliveries increase in number. When environmentalists attack industries for polluting the environment, the industries respond with more toxic waste. It is simply the law of balance and counterbalance in the physical world.

It is not that established institutions can never be changed. It is only that you cannot use the darkness of the human world to produce something of light. You cannot try to fix something with the very parts that are broken and meet with any success. If and when people are repaired and reconnected to the spiritual world, they will then have the weapons and resources to combat the human world.

Because of education's position in society, it could only be stopped immediately by some major interruption in Western social life. It would take a major natural disaster or a serious nuclear accident or war to stop modern education. It would take something so powerful that all normal daily living would be completely interrupted and people would be forced to shift their focus from human success to simple survival.

The only thing that people in Western societies can do to begin to restore their own planet is to find a way to repair their current damages and straighten out their accumulated incorrect ideas.

There are very few ways to accomplish this without the Brotherhood's help. Most are very long and tedious at best.

Several hundred years ago, the Brotherhood inspired the authors of the American Bill of Rights. Through the Bill of Rights the Brotherhood was able to give humanity specific ideas and impressions about personal freedom and individual rights. Today, over 200 years later, nations throughout the world still use the Bill of Rights as a model for their own constitutions. Over 150 countries have picked up the ideas of personal freedom and individual rights. Each of these nations expresses those ideas in its own unique way. Most have not yet discovered how to translate these ideas into everyday life. However, people are working on it and that is a good start.

This book and the others in this series, like the Bill of Rights, have been given to humanity in order to establish certain ideas and impressions about souls, and about why people are alive. We do not expect that people will begin to live by these ideas, or that they will even understand what these ideas and impressions mean. As with the Bill of Rights, people someday will pick up on these ideas and impressions. It will be many centuries before people can translate these ideas into everyday life. However, anyone who reads this book has already begun to work on it—whether they like it or not—and that is a good start.

It would be a very serious mistake for someone to think that We are trying to tell parents to pull their children out of schools, or to use this material as the basis for an alternative system. We are not attempting to do either. In fact, the material contained in this book only begins to describe an interim educational system, one that would bridge the gap between the current system and the one from which humanity could aetually benefit. People are far too damaged to be able to march directly into the "promised land" of school systems.

This interim system would be similar to, although not exactly like, A. S. Neill's "Summerhill." This interim system would have to be in place for at least five generations before humanity would be capable of using the type of long-term educational system We would propose. After five generations, even great-great-grandparents would only remember this interim system, and the scars of the current educational institution would be at least partially washed away.

Even this interim system would have its difficulties. All current languages as they exist cause people to use the left brain hemisphere or linear mind. It is much more natural for people to communicate in ideas portrayed in symbols than it is to use current languages. The Japanese and the Chinese made an attempt at establishing such a communication system with simple symbols, but because of the darkness the system failed. Now both Japanese and Chinese languages have become so cumbersome and complicated that even scholars have difficulty understanding them.

In the future, humanity will have, by necessity, a universal language. It will be a system of 128 symbols which will represent ideas rather than words and sentences. These ideas will be read from top to bottom on a page since this is the most natural way for a person to read. It will be a universal system because people will find it necessary to develop some means of world-wide communication, and they will be compelled by their own advancement to develop a system which allows linear communication to occur in a non-linear way. People will see clearly that current languages are actually destructive, simply because of the nature of their construction.

Until that time comes, people will always suffer a certain amount of damage as a result of the linear language systems. Our interim school system would only serve as a stopgap to prevent the kind of destruction that now occurs from education. For instance, the interim system would prevent people from giving anything to children to study or memorize before the age of eight or nine. This alone would stop an enormous amount of damage. Children would be protected from mental destruction during this time when they are most vulnerable. These interim schools could be likened to constructing a safe containment system for nuclear waste (which humanity does not know how to do). The nuclear waste would still be deadly but it would be confined to areas that could not severely damage or even destroy the human race. These interim schools would contain the toxicity of schools. However, they would not in any way guarantee that the planet would be preserved from harm.

Education, like nuclear waste, has no safe containment system today. It is spilling out all over humanity without any controls. In some ways, it would be easier for the human race if people physically destroyed most of this planet and then rebuilt from scratch. This has been done before on more than one occasion and has met with success.

Now any attempts to rebuild the planet automatically meet with failure, especially regarding modern education. At the risk of being offensive, modern education is like a giant toilet. Whenever people try to put a good idea into it, the system flushes the idea away. Open classrooms were a good idea that went into a toilet and got flushed away. Summerhill demonstrated some very good ideas and they have all been flushed away. Occasionally, there are good people who sincerely want to teach children, and they get flushed away. The educational system is such a big toilet that it can handle a limitless number of good ideas and well-meaning people by flushing all of them away. It may take a few tries, but sooner or later anything good in the educational system is bound to be destroyed, which is why We are not advocating that anyone try to change this system without the resources to do it.

Our purpose in offering this book is only to jolt and to shock people back into reality. People who have read this book will soon slip back into unconsciousness. It will take many books and repeated efforts before humanity can tolerate enough reality to begin restoring this planet. We can only plant the seeds so that many years from now maybe, just maybe, some will grow.

To obtain information about the work of Gentle Wind and about other books in this series, you may call or write:

Gentle Wind Retreat
P.O. Box 184
Surry, ME 04684

1-207-374-5478

(Calling hours are between 9:00 A.M. and 7:00 P.M. daily.)